Biblical Women—Submissive?

Biblical Women—Submissive?

JOE E. LUNCEFORD

WIPF & STOCK · Eugene, Oregon

BIBLICAL WOMEN—SUBMISSIVE?

Copyright © 2009 Joe E. Lunceford. All rights reserved. Except for brief quotations in critical publications or reviews, no part of this book may be reproduced in any manner without prior written permission from the publisher. Write: Permissions, Wipf and Stock Publishers, 199 W. 8th Ave., Suite 3, Eugene, OR 97401.

Wipf & Stock
An imprint of Wipf and Stock Publishers
199 W. 8th Ave., Suite 3
Eugene, OR 97401

www.wipfandstock.com

ISBN 13: 978-1-60608-178-5

Manufactured in the U.S.A.

*To my best friend, my lover, my partner in ministry,
my companion, my constant encourager, my wife*

Rev. Stacey DeAnn Cruse

*this work is lovingly dedicated. She has taught me much concerning the
mutual submission of husbands and wives to one another.*

Contents

Acknowledgments / xi
Abbreviations / xii
Introduction / xiii

PART ONE: Named Women

1. Sarai/Sarah / 3
2. Rebekah / 7
3. Rachel and Leah / 9
4. Dinah / 12
5. Tamar / 15
6. Some General Comments / 19
7. Zipporah / 21
8. Shiphrah and Puah / 24
9. Miriam / 25
10. Mahlah, Noah, Hoglah, Milcah, and Tirzah / 28
11. Rahab / 29
12. Achsah / 34
13. Deborah / 36
14. Jael / 42
15. Sheerah / 46
16. Ruth / 48
17. Naomi / 54
18. Abigail / 56

Contents

19	Michal / 59	
20	Bathsheba / 64	
21	Jezebel / 70	
22	Athaliah / 76	
23	Huldah / 79	
24	Noadiah / 84	
25	Vashti / 86	
26	Esther / 89	
27	Anna / 92	
28	Mary, Mother of Jesus / 95	
29	Mary Magdalene / 98	
30	Martha and Mary of Bethany / 104	
31	Mary, Mother of John Mark / 109	
32	Joanna / 111	
33	Prisca/Priscilla / 114	
34	Phoebe / 119	
35	Junia/Julia / 125	
36	Euodia and Syntyche / 128	
37	Lydia / 130	
38	Tryphaena and Tryphosa / 133	
39	Nympha / 135	
40	Apphia / 137	

PART TWO: Unnamed Women

41	Manoah's Wife / 143	
42	The Heroine of Thebez / 145	
43	The Medium of En-dor / 147	
44	The Wise Woman of Tekoa / 150	
45	The Wise Woman of Abel Beth-maacah / 154	

Contents

46 The Queen of Sheba / 156
47 The Shunnamite Woman / 159
48 The Wife of Isaiah / 163
49 The Idealized Woman of Proverbs 31 / 165
50 The Samaritan Woman / 170
51 The Woman and the Unjust Judge / 175
52 The Woman Who Anointed Jesus / 177
53 The Elect Lady / 180
54 Philip's Daughters / 183

Bibliography / 187

Acknowledgments

First of all, I would like to thank the Administration of Georgetown College for granting me a sabbatical during which most of the writing of this book was done. I would also like to thank my colleagues in the Religion Department of Georgetown College, Drs. Paul Redditt, Lydia Hoyle, Jeffrey Asher, Jack Birdwhistell, and Sheila Klopfer for their support, their encouragement, and assistance with this work. I am deeply indebted to all who have had a part in teaching me a love for the Bible and have opened my eyes to new possibilities of meaning in its text. These include, but are no means limited to, Drs. Ray Frank Robbins, Robert Soileau, J. Hardee Kennedy, Thomas J. Delaughter, J. Wash Watts, Ray Summers, Eddie Dwyer, and Henry Jackson Flanders, Jr. Others, such as Drs. Rex Ray Pearce and Clayton Waddell, have taught me much from their expertise in ethics and sociology concerning the equality of the sexes and the many ways in which women have received unequal treatment in our society.

I would also like to acknowledge that the materials in the chapters on Sarah, Rachel and Leah, Deborah, Sheerah, Huldah, Anna, Priscilla, Phoebe, and Junia were originally published in the Fall 2000 issue of Priscilla Papers, the scholarly journal of the Christians for Biblical Equality organization, with a few minor revisions.

Last, but not least, I express my gratitude to editors Diane Farley and Christian Amondson of Wipf and Stock Publishers, without whose assistance this work would not have been published.

Abbreviations

ASV	American Standard Version
BCE	Before the Common Era
CE	Common Era
DRV	Douai-Rheims Version
KJV	King James Version
LNT	Living New Testament
NAB	New American Bible
NASB	New American Standard Bible
NEB	New English Bible
NIV	New International Version
NRSV	New Revised Standard Version
REB	Revised English Bible
RSV	Revised Standard Version
TEV	Today's English Version
TNIV	Today's New International Version
TNT	The New Translation

Introduction

I SUPPOSE FROM THE time I became old enough to think for myself I have always had something of a feminist streak in me. I can remember arguing with my classmates in the seventh grade that men, as well as women, should learn how to cook! To be completely honest, at that point in my development I still assumed that women should do the cooking and other housework unless they were incapacitated in some way. My argument then was simply that women *do* get sick, and therefore men should be prepared to take over the housework. Even with this caveat, I was notoriously unsuccessful in swaying my classmates to my point of view.

I have come a long way in my thinking in the approximately fifty-five years since my experience recounted above. I have become aware that women have been discriminated against severely in many different ways and in many different areas of life. Having been an ordained Baptist minister for the past forty-nine years, I have come to see that the church in its many forms has more often been in the role of oppressor than of liberator. In particular, the Bible has been used to relegate women to a second-class status (or worse, sometimes) in Christian circles. I have also come to the conclusion that faulty methods of interpretation of the Bible are largely responsible for this situation, and that, when properly interpreted, the Bible contains a message of liberation of *all* people from *all* that diminishes their freedom to become all that God has made them capable of becoming. As Tikva Frymer-Kensky has said so well, "But when we look at the Bible, we find something very interesting. In a patriarchal world where men were the major actors, in a world where women were not so much shackled as they were limited by the felt need to control their sexuality, despite all of the androcentric focus in the Bible, women keep cropping up as figures from the margin who know what should happen and do whatever is necessary to make sure it happens."[1] I have attempted

---

1. Tikva Frymer-Kensky, "Goddesses: Biblical Echoes," 43.

Introduction

to bring some of these women from the margins to the forefront and highlight what they accomplished.

I had been a lifelong Southern Baptist until about three years ago when the church of which I am now a member pulled out of the Southern Baptist Convention, primarily over the issue of the freedom of women to exercise their God-given calls to ministry without limitations. There were other issues, to be sure, but this one was at the top of the list. When the Convention issued its (in)famous resolution that all women should be "graciously submissive" to their husbands I decided I could no longer keep silent (actually I had been discussing this issue very openly in the classroom for twenty-odd years before this). My first public response outside the classroom was to deliver a lecture, and later publish an article in the Fall 2000 issue of *Priscilla Papers*, the scholarly journal of Christians for Biblical Equality, with the title, "Biblical Women Weren't always Submissive." That article, with no substantive changes, is a part of this book. I have continued to read and research this issue in all the intervening years. It is out of these experiences that this book was born.

This book attempts to make a comprehensive study of all the women of the Bible, both named and unnamed, who have either defied the roles assigned them by the system of patriarchy or whose lives have not been defined in terms of a husband or other male in their lives. I approach the passages in the Bible where the stories of these women are found with a "hermeneutics of suspicion," to use a term made famous by Elizabeth Schussler Fiorenza in the 1980s.[2] Wherever possible, I refer to elements of later Christian tradition that suggest an increased role of the woman in question, beyond what her story in the Bible reflects. For the most part I restrict myself to the stories as they appear in the Bible, but I often suggest how there might be more to the story than we are told. I sometimes speculate as to how many women's stories may have been deliberately squelched by male authors and religious leaders.

I have consciously written in a manner that will appeal to the scholar as well as to the non-scholar. To that end, I have relegated any technical issues to the notes, for the most part, so that any informed reader can read the text and skip over the technical issues if they wish. At all points, I have given due credit to the sources from which I have drawn my ideas.

---

2. Fiorenza, *In Memory of Her*, xxiii.

Introduction

I have not rigidly followed any sort of order in which these women are considered. I first deal with the named women, then the unnamed women, in first the Jewish Scriptures, then the Christian Testament. To the degree possible, I have tried to keep these women in roughly the chronological order in which they appear. This study would be unaffected by any different order in which they might be considered.

One of my colleagues has issued the famous dictum that when you publish anything, start ducking! I am taking his advice at this point. To the more conservative I will appear too liberal. To the more liberal I will appear too conservative. I am actually quite comfortable with being considered a "middle-of-the-roader." To suggest that all the truth belongs to any one church system, theological stance, or philosophical system is to claim more than any human being has a right to claim.

I am far beyond the point of being greatly affected by any label that someone may place on me. As far as I am concerned, the question, Is this conservative? or, Is this liberal? are meaningless. The only question worth asking is, Is it *truth*? That is the only question I am interested in considering. I have attempted to let that question govern this study from start to finish. My good friend and former professor, the late Ray Summers, defined research as "following truth wherever it leads."[3] That made a permanent impression on me, and this is the way I have approached research since I first heard him speak those words.

I neither expect nor desire that all who read this book will agree with me. If I have raised a few new questions, or suggested new ideas to some readers, or have opened the eyes of any to new possibilities, I will have accomplished my goal.

---

3. Ray Summers, classroom lecture, 1975.

PART ONE

Named Women

1

Sarai/Sarah

According to the Biblical story the wife of Abraham was originally named Sarai ("contentious one"). At the point where God made a covenant with Abraham, her name was changed to Sarah ("princess") [Gen 17:15]. The Christian Testament author of 1 Peter exhorts his female readers to be submissive to their husbands, invoking as an example Sarah who "obeyed Abraham, calling him *kyrios* ("lord") [1 Pet 3:1–6]." *Kyrios* is roughly the equivalent of the Hebrew *baal*. However, as Carol Meyers has noted, "the absolute sovereignty of one person over another is expressed (in Hebrew) not by *ba'al* but by another word, *'adon* ("lord"), as in the control of a conqueror over the vanquished or of a master over the slave."[1] Hence both Sarah's alleged obedience and the title used in addressing Abraham require further examination.

It is true that, at the point where Sarah and Abraham are promised a son in their old age, Sarah refers to Abraham as my *baal* ("lord") [Gen 18:12]. In context, however, this title probably means nothing more than "husband."[2] When the translators of the Greek version of the Jewish Scriptures rendered *baal* as *kyrios* in this passage, they opened up an even broader set of possibilities of meaning. *Kyrios* may convey anything from a polite "sir" or "mister" to the idea of God or Jesus Christ as being the supreme authority for one's life.[3] Upon closer examination, therefore, Sarah's reference to Abraham as *baal* has no necessary connection with her obedience to him. In fact, as Nunnally-Cox has noted, "There does seem to be a surprising amount of equality between Sarah and Abraham.

---

1. Carol Meyers, *Discovering Eve*, 182.
2. *Theological Dictionary of the Old Testament*, 1977 ed., s.v. "baal."
3. *Greek-English Lexicon of the New Testament Based upon Semantic Domains*, s.v. "kyrios."

She appears to say what she wants, when she wants, and Abraham at times responds in almost meek obedience."[4]

When we examine the complete Biblical story of Abraham and Sarah, we see rather quickly that the author of 1 Peter has used the reference to Abraham as *baal* in a very dubious manner. His interpretation is apparently tinged with hero/heroine worship.[5] Let us take a closer look at that story.

The Biblical promise to Abraham and Sarah that they would have a son in their old age is so well known as not to require comment. When faced with the apparent impossibility of the fulfillment of this promise, Sarah took matters into her own hands by *directing* Abraham to go in and have sexual relations with her maid Hagar (Gen 16:2). Regardless of how this might appear to us in modern times, Sarah was probably following a custom that was commonplace in her world. Excavations between 1925 and 1931 at Nuzi, an ancient city on the Tigris River in northern Mesopotamia, produced a large find of clay tablets that reflect this custom, along with several others that appear elsewhere in the Bible.[6] According to the Biblical story, Nuzi is in the general area from which Abraham came (Gen 11:27–31; 15:7)

From this relationship between Abraham and Hagar a son was born whom they named Ishmael (Gen 16:11). Although some English translations render this in such a way as to leave the impression that Sarah is only requesting Abraham to go in to Hagar (e.g., NASB, KJV, ASV), both the Hebrew and Greek texts suggest otherwise. According to the English text of Genesis 16:2, Abram (Abraham) *listened* to the voice of Sarah. The word "listened" translates the Hebrew word *shema*, which is rendered by *hypakouō* in the Greek version of the Hebrew Bible. As any standard lexicon will show, both the Hebrew and the Greek word are regularly used in the sense of not only hearing, but obeying what is heard.[7] This usage is the only one that makes sense in the larger context of Genesis 16:2. To put the matter as simply as possible, Sarah spoke and Abraham obeyed—just as countless husbands have done all down through the centuries. Parales has commented further, "Sarah held great authority within her family unit. In

---

4. Nunnally-Cox, *Foremothers*, 9.
5. Cf. Scanzoni and Hardesty, *All We're Meant to Be*, 140–44.
6. *Mercer Dictionary of the Bible*, s.v. "Nuzi."
7. Cf. Trible, *Texts of Terror*, 11.

fact, her authority was great enough that at one point God commanded Abraham to obey her (Gen 21:12).

After Hagar bore Ishmael, she began to taunt Sarah for her barrenness (Gen 16:5). Sarah, regretting that she had given Hagar to Abraham, wanted to send away both Hagar and Ishmael. Abraham's response was to give Sarah permission to do whatever she wished to Hagar, and Sarah drove her and Ishmael away. "Sarah demonstrated that she was no inferior, submissive female."[8]

Trible, in her comments on this story, makes the initiative of Sarah more pointed: "No mighty Patriarch Abram, but rather the silent, acquiescent, and minor figure in a drama between two women."[9] Although this may be a slight overstatement, it is probably closer to reality than what we read in 1 Peter.

As we follow the Abraham story, some thirteen years after Ishmael's birth Sarah gave birth to a son they named Isaac. Predictably, family problems arose very soon because of the two sons. Soon after Isaac's birth Sarah saw Ishmael, who appears to have been a teenager by this time (Gen 17:25), "mocking" Isaac. Exactly what Ishmael was doing cannot be determined precisely. The word "mocking" translates the Hebrew word *shachaq* and the Greek word *paizō*. The Hebrew word, interestingly, is the root word for the name Issac, which means "laughter" (cf. Gen 21:6). The implication may be either laughing *with* Ishmael or laughing *at* him. John Skinner has suggested that the scene of the two children playing together without regard for social distinctions excited a maternal jealousy in Sarah.[10] Wenham correctly notes that this places Sarah in a negative light. He suggests as a more likely possibility that Ishmael was making fun of Isaac's status and of the circumstances of his birth; and Sarah saw Ishmael as playing the role of Isaac.[11] Although both of these suggestions are possible, this may be nothing more than an ancient story of sibling rivalry. Older siblings harassing younger ones is probably as old as the human race. We are on firmer ground in taking note that whatever Ishmael may have been doing clearly displeased Sarah. She immediately went to Abraham with the *demand*, "Drive out this maid and her son, for the son

---

8. Parales, *Hidden Voices*, 20.
9. Ibid.
10. Cited in Hubbard and Barker, gen. eds., *Genesis 16–50*, 82.
11. Ibid.

of this maid shall not be an heir with my son Isaac" (Gen 21:10, NASB).[12] So much for Sarah's obedience to Abraham—for the second time Sarah spoke and *Abraham* obeyed. And if one should point out that in the latter case God commanded Abraham to do as Sarah demanded (Gen 21:12), this is even more damaging to the popular chauvinistic claim that the Bible teaches unqualified submission and obedience of women to their husbands. Abraham did not make the choice in this instance, but God *commanded* him to obey Sarah.

Lest anyone miss the obvious here, Abraham was no ordinary, commonplace citizen of the ancient world. He is looked to as the father of three world religions: Islam, Judaism, and Christianity.

---

12. I am keenly aware of the injustice done to Hagar in this story. To discuss that issue is beyond the scope of this study, however. For anyone interested in pursuing Hagar's story I would refer her/him to Trible, *Texts of Terror*, 9–29.

2

Rebekah

THE STORY OF ISAAC and his wife Rebekah presents a situation in which the woman does not openly and obviously dictate what her husband should do, but who just as surely took charge of circumstances and controlled their outcome on occasion. Furthermore, in doing so she altered permanently the history of the descendants of Abraham. Rebekah gave birth to twins, Jacob and Esau. Esau was a hunter, a "man's man," and because of this was beloved of his father. Jacob, on the other hand, stayed close to his mother's tent and was Rebekah's favorite (Gen 25:27–28). Esau was born first, and was therefore the one who was entitled to receive the birthright and the blessing of his father. The birthright entitled the recipient to receive a double portion of the family inheritance and the position of leadership of the family, among other things.[1]

One day Esau came home from a hunting trip and was famished. Jacob happened to be cooking a savory stew, and Esau asked Jacob to share it with him. Jacob agreed to do so—in return for Esau's birthright! Esau agreed, saying the birthright wouldn't mean much to him if he starved to death (Gen 25:29–34). This bargain secured the birthright for Jacob, but getting the blessing of his father was another matter. This Rebekah would secure for him.

As Isaac realized he was nearing the time of his death, and his eyes were too dim to see much of anything, he instructed his son Esau to go hunting and bring back wild game and prepare it in the way that Isaac loved. Rebekah overheard these instructions and promptly called Jacob to her. At this point Rebekah actively took control of matters. She set forth a plan to have Jacob carry savory food that she had prepared to Isaac while pretending to be Esau to receive the blessing. Because Esau was

---

1. *The International Standard Bible Encyclopedia*, 1956 ed., s.v. "Birthright."

a hairy man and Jacob was smooth, Rebekah dressed Jacob in some of Esau's clothing and wrapped the skins of young goats around his hands (Gen 27:1–21). Isaac seemed to be a bit suspicious, saying the hands were the hands of Esau, but the voice was Jacob's (Gen 27:22); the deception worked, however, and Isaac bestowed the blessing upon Jacob. When Esau came in and learned of the deception, he asked Isaac to bless him also. Isaac indicated that the blessing of Jacob could not be reversed (Gen 27:33), and that Esau would be his brother's servant; but he did give a lesser blessing to Esau (Gen 27:34–40).

Needless to say, Esau was not happy with this turn of events. He vowed that after the death and burial of his father he would kill his brother Jacob. Once more, Rebekah took charge. She managed to have Isaac send Jacob to the land of Haran to her brother Laban, pretending that she wanted him to find a wife from her own people instead of marrying one of the local women as Esau had done (twice; see Gen 26:34).

Rebekah drops out of the story at this point. The only other reference to her that has survived is the account of her being buried in the family burial ground (Gen 49:31). The summary of her life by Nunnally-Cox merits our close attention. "Rebekah, we would have to say, does not stay innocently beautiful long, for she grows from the water-girl into a powerful, influential matriarch. It is interesting to note that the writer does not judge her behavior; he simply tells her story. Her influence over Jacob and Isaac is evident: both seem to do her bidding, with little or no protest. Rebekah appears to be a master of Intrigue, and has learned well to have her way. She is strong and daring and bold, not at all cast in a submissive mold, her spirit willful and very much alive."[2]

---

2. Nunnally-Cox, *Foremothers*, 15.

3

Rachel and Leah

I HAVE CHOSEN TO consider Rachel and Leah together, because their stories as wives of the patriarch Jacob are so intertwined as to make separation virtually impossible. As I noted earlier, Jacob had, with the encouragement and assistance of his mother Rebekah, swindled Esau out of his birthright and his father's blessing. Upon learning that Esau had vowed to kill Jacob, Rebekah sent him to the land of Haran to find a wife, under the pretext that she was afraid he would marry one of the local Canaanite women (as Esau had done) (Gen 27:1—28:2).

Upon arrival in Haran, Jacob sought out Laban, his mother's brother, and met Laban's daughter Rachel at a well where his flocks were watered. Apparently it was a Biblical example of "love at first sight" (cf. Gen 28:5-20), and Jacob agreed to serve Laban for seven years in exchange for Rachel's hand in marriage. At the end of the seven years, however, Jacob discovered too late that he had been given Leah instead of Rachel (the eastern custom of brides being veiled as they entered into the bridal chamber would explain how Jacob could be fooled in this manner). When Jacob confronted Laban with the deception, he gave the lame excuse that it was not customary to give a younger daughter in marriage before the older (Gen 29:26). He then "generously" offered to give Jacob Rachel as well—in exchange for another seven years of service (Gen 29:27). (One of my college professors was fond of saying that Jacob paid cash for Leah, but bought Rachel on the installment plan!) Laban also gave Bilhah to Rachel as her maid (Gen 29:29).

As we follow the story we find that Rachel was always Jacob's favorite, and this situation became highly problematic in the family. This was largely due to the fact that Leah was the fertile wife, giving Jacob no less than six sons and one daughter (Gen 29:31-37; 30:17-21). Rachel seems to have blamed Jacob for her inability to bear children and confronted him accordingly (Gen 30:1–2). Jacob, in accordance with a belief attested at numerous points in the Bible, asserted that God, not he, had withheld children from Rachel (Gen 30:2).

The next development is that Rachel gave her maid Bilhah to Jacob to bear children for her. Once more, because we are so far removed from the world of ancient Mesopotamia, this strikes us as more than a little strange; but, like Sarah before her, she was probably following a widely accepted custom of that day.

Rachel's plan was successful, and Bilhah bore Jacob two sons (Gen 30:5–8). When Leah saw this, she followed suit and gave her maid Zilpah to Jacob as a wife. Zilpah likewise bore Jacob two sons (Gen 30:9–13).

The story took a new and surprising twist when one day Reuben, Leah's oldest son, brought home some "mandrakes" he had found in a field. Exactly what sort of plants these were is uncertain, but since at least the third century BCE they have been commonly interpreted as a stemless perennial plant called *mandragora officinarum* or *atropa mandragora*, which was common in the eastern Mediterranean world.[1] Although not commonly grown for food, the roots and berries of this plant are edible.[2] The plant was most prized in the ancient world, however, for its alleged qualities as a fertility drug and an aphrodisiac; and these qualities are clearly pivotal in the Jacob story. Rachel asked Leah to share her son's mandrakes and was met with the testy response, "Is it a small matter for you to take my husband? And would you take my son's mandrakes also (Gen 30:15)?" Rachel then "generously" offered to allow Leah to have Jacob for the night in return for some of the mandrakes. (I will resist the temptation to comment upon the status to which this reduces Jacob, but it takes no great intellect to figure that out!) Niditch has no such reservations, and spells it out: "Jacob is the hired lover, told with whom he will lie."[3] I will restrict my own comments to the obvious fact that Leah spoke and Jacob obeyed, just as his grandfather had done in the Abraham story.

Once again I would point out that we are not dealing with a person of any ordinary status, but him whose name was changed to Israel (Gen 32:28) and who gave that name permanently to the covenant people of God in the Jewish Scriptures.

1. Hubbard and Barker, gen. eds., *Genesis 16–50*, 246. Cf. also *Harper's Bible Dictionary*, s.v. "Mandrake"; and *Mercer Dictionary of the Bible*, s.v. "Mandrake."
2. *Holman Bible Dictionary*, s.v. "Mandrake."
3. Niditch, "Eroticism and Death in the Tale of Jael," 49.

Rachel and Leah

Perhaps a summary comment on these two women is in order. In the words of Nunnally-Cox, "These women, these matriarchs, are once again bold, daring and astounding in their lack of obedience. Fathers and husbands may have rule, but the women have power, and they use it to best advantage."[4]

With Leah and Rachel the history of the legendary matriarchs comes to a close. Far from conforming to a traditional servitude, these women grace the pages of Genesis with their laughter, their sorrows, their strength, and their power."[5]

---

4. Nunnally-Cox, *Foremothers*, 20.
5. Ibid.

4

Dinah

AT FIRST GLANCE IT may appear strange that I have included Dinah in this discussion. Her story as we have it in the Jewish Scriptures seems to be one of a female being systematically exploited by the men in her family. Certainly the story is that—but there are a couple of things that make me suspicious we are not getting anything like the whole story. The major difficulty is that, as with much of the Jewish Scriptures (and the Christian Testament as well), the voice of the female is suppressed. We get not one word from Dinah as to how *she* saw the situation.

As we look at the story in Genesis 34, Dinah is said to have gone out to visit the "daughters of the land" (Gen 34:1). She is spotted by Shechem, one of the local Hivites, who rapes her, according to the text (Gen 34:2). Then Shechem begs his father Hamor to get Dinah for him as a wife (Gen 34:3-4). Word reaches Jacob concerning the rape of his daughter Dinah, and her brothers are incensed that this "foreigner" has raped their sister (Gen 34:5-7). Hamor then meets with Jacob and his sons, asking them that Dinah be given to his son as a wife and offering a general intermarrying between the Hivite people and Jacob's family. (Note the matter-of-fact way in which such intermarriage is attested in Judges 3:5-6, although such liaisons are warned against in other passages of the Jewish Scriptures, notably Exodus 34:10-16.) Hamor offers to pay whatever bridal price they may ask of him. Jacob and his sons agree to this, on the condition that the Hivites submit to circumcision (Gen 34:9-17). Hamor and Shechem agree to these terms and waste no time in submitting to the circumcision "because he (Shechem) was delighted with Jacob's daughter" (Gen 34:19b). On the third day after the circumcision Simeon and Levi, sons of Jacob, went to the "city" of the Hivites and treacherously killed every male, including Hamor and Shechem, and looted their village (Gen 34:25-30).

Dinah

They then took their sister Dinah back home. Thus ends the story of Dinah as we have it in the Bible.

So what can there possibly be in this story that reflects a female as stepping out of her cultural role and acting in less than a submissive manner to the males in her life? The first red flag I see is in the opening verse of Genesis 34. Dinah went out to visit the "daughters of the land." Did she get the permission of her father and/or her brothers? The story does not say. This alone might suggest that Dinah was a headstrong young woman, determined to find her own way in the world. Furthermore, Dinah would not be the last teenager to claim to be going out to visit with her female friends when her real motive was to scope out the boys in the area! (I am assuming the age of Dinah was somewhere between fourteen and sixteen because of the general tendency of women to marry shortly after puberty in the ancient world.[1]) I am suggesting that Dinah may have had the same sort of feelings for Shechem that he had for her, and that instead of rape we may have a consensual sexual encounter.[2] Sue and Larry Richards hint at this possibility, although they do seem to accept what happened to Dinah as rape. "We are not told anything about Dinah's feelings. Was she glad to be rescued, or had she fallen in love with Shechem?"[3] This would have been very damaging to the male members of her family, indicating that they were unable to control their women. Second, I would point out that Dinah would have been unable to admit to a consensual sexual encounter with Shechem without endangering her life (cf. the story of Tamar and Judah in Gen 38:12–34).These would be ample motives for a male author to have covered up the real details of this story.

The other detail of the story that I see as support for my speculations is that after the "rape," Shechem asserts his love for Dinah in the strongest of terms (Gen 34:2–3). This is not what one would expect of a rapist. The usual pattern would be for the rapist to treat the victim with the utmost contempt after the rape (cf. the story of Amnon's rape of Tamar in 2 Sam 13:1–22 and Phyllis Trible, *Texts of Terror*, 46–48.). This kind of detail is

---

1. See, for example, *Mercer Dictionary of the Bible*, s.v. "Marriage in the Old Testament."

2. A small point in favor of this suggestion is that the RSV gives as the heading of the biblical story of Dinah as "The Seduction of Dinah." And, in the words of Nunnally-Cox (*Foremothers*, 22), "Seduction implies that Dinah had a part or at least a choice in the matter, yet the story gives no indication of this."

3. Richards and Richards, *Every Woman*, 25.

precisely the sort of thing that often results from the deliberate changing of some details of a story in order to cover up something that would have been damaging to male participants in the story. Unfortunately, we can never hear the voice of Dinah in this story, but if we could I suspect we would get a lot of new details that would give the story a very different slant. In the end I must confess that what I have suggested here has to be left in the realm of speculation—but I will argue that it is very plausible speculation. I will further confess the possibility that I have been unduly influenced by Anita Diamant's bestselling novel,[4] but I will leave that for the reader to judge.

---

4. Diamont, *The Red Tent*.

5

Tamar

THIS TAMAR IS NOT to be confused with a daughter of David, whose story is told in 2 Samuel 13:1–32, or with a daughter of Absalom, who is briefly mentioned in 2 Samuel 14:27. She is the daughter-in-law of the patriarch Judah, from whose lineage the Messiah was expected to come.

Tamar's story is told in Genesis 38:1–30. It interrupts the story of Joseph being sold into slavery in Egypt and his rise to power in that land. Both chronologically and textually it fits in very poorly. It appears that at least twenty years would be required for the described events to take place, and the story of Jacob and his sons does not seem to allow for such a period of time.[1] For those interested in such critical questions, the reader is referred to Petersen's account of the story of Tamar and Judah.[2] I will deal with the story on its own merits, as it appears in Genesis 38.

The story begins with Judah's departing from his family and marrying a Canaanite woman named Shua, who bore him three sons: Er, Onan, and Shelah (38:1–5). When Er became of marriageable age, Judah took for him a wife named Tamar (v. 6). We are not told how long this marriage lasted, only that Er was evil in the sight of the Lord and the Lord killed him (v. 7). Judah then commands Onan to fulfill his levirate (from Latin *levir*, "brother-in-law") duty and marry Tamar for the purpose of raising an offspring for his brother (v. 8). Onan was clearly not happy with this arrangement, knowing that the child born would not be his, and so he practiced *coitus interruptus*, spilling his seed on the ground each time he cohabited with Tamar (v. 9). The Biblical narrator tells us that this displeased the Lord; so he killed Onan also (v. 10). Now Judah is left with only one son, the young Shelah. Judah orders Tamar

---

1. Petersen, *Reading Women's Stories*, 120.
2. Ibid., 119–64.

to return to her father's house to wait until Shelah grew up. His real motivation, however, was to make sure that Shelah did not suffer the same fate as his two brothers (v. 11). In doing so, "Not only did he deny Tamar her right to a levirate marriage, but he also neglected to perform the ceremony of *halizah,* which would have released Tamar from the levirate bond so she could freely marry another."[3] In Berquist's words, "She could not marry anyone else, because she was legally bound to Judah's family and to the eldest unmarried male. Judah was cheating according to the law by withholding Shelah from her, but there was apparently nothing she could do. Women did not have the power to force a man's hand on an issue such as this."[4]

In the next story development, Judah's wife dies and, after a period of mourning, Judah returns to normal activities. He heads for Timnah along with his friend Hiram the Adullamite to shear his sheep (v. 12). By this time Tamar has apparently recognized that Shelah would never become her husband, so she takes matters into her own hands. Upon learning that Judah is on the way to Timnah, she veiled herself and waited by the road he was traveling. Judah, thinking Tamar was a prostitute, propositioned her immediately. When she asked what he would give her as payment, he promised her a kid from his flocks. Obviously he did not have a kid with him at the time, so Tamar asked for a security deposit; namely for his seal, his cord (sash), and his staff (vv. 13–18). (One scholar has compared having these items with having all of someone's credit cards in modern times.)[5] Tamar then changed into her widow's clothing and went home (v. 19).

Three months later Judah is told that Tamar has "played the harlot" and is pregnant. Upon hearing this, he immediately commands that she be brought out and burned (v. 24). "It couldn't have made Judah happier, because now he had the chance to finish this problem once and for all. Since she had clearly been unfaithful and had violated her widowhood, she had lost all of her rights to his precious Shelah. Judah served as prosecutor, judge, and jury. Tamar must die."[6] This was an extreme punishment, even for adultery. Leviticus 21:9 provides for this punishment for the daughter

---

3. Miriam Therese Winter, *Tamar.*

4. Berquist, *Reclaiming Her Story,* 74.

5. Hubbard and Barker, gen. eds., *Genesis 16–50,* 367. Cf. also Berquist *Reclaiming Her Story,* 74.

6. Ibid., 74–75.

Tamar

of a priest, but nowhere in the Jewish Scriptures is this prescribed for everyone who happened to commit adultery.

Tamar is powerless and defenseless in the light of the power of the patriarch—or is she? As she is being brought out to be burned she sends Judah's seal, his cord, and his staff, saying that their owner was the man who got her pregnant (v. 25). When asked if he recognized them, Judah (to his credit) acclaimed Tamar as being more righteous than he, in that he had refused to allow her to marry Shelah (v. 26). The story concludes with Tamar's giving birth to twins, thus continuing the family line.

This story, like many in the Jewish Scriptures, is subject to more than one reading.

Is this just another misogynist text in which females are mere pawns in the hands of the males who control their fate? Or, might we turn this around and ask who the real pawn is in the story. A possible answer is that Judah is the one who fits that description. To be sure, Tamar has no overt power and has to resort to trickery and deception. She nevertheless controls the outcome of the story and ensures the continuation of the lineage that would produce King David and, according to the belief of many, the Messiah. This is no small feat. Touching on the various roles Tamar has played in this story, Berquist writes, "Tamar the trickster, Tamar the spurned, Tamar the prostitute, Tamar the incestuous is Tamar the righteous.... Female power is exalted, not denied.... Female righteousness, in violation of all sense of order, defeated the male power and control that threatened to snuff out Tamar's possibilities for life."[7] As Rendsburg has noted, "Tamar serves as God's agent here, exacting punishment on the sinful male dominators and tricksters of the Book of Genesis."[8]

Petersen has provided a fitting conclusion to the discussion of Tamar's roles and character: "she is in a sense the heroine of the story. Although she is only 'a poor, diminished female,' the role she plays defines 'a new understanding of righteousness.' She becomes the only woman in the Bible who is declared righteous.... Unlike Leah, who is passive and manipulated by Laban, Tamar is the sole arbiter of her own fate, the prime mover and protagonist of her own story."[9] Lest the reader miss the deep paradox here, I would point out that a "powerless" woman, victimized by

---

7. Ibid., 75–76.
8. Rendsburg, "Unlikely Heroes," 53.
9. Petersen, *Reading Women's Stories*, 153.

a thoroughly patriarchal society and who openly practices lying, deceit, and manipulation, has become the only woman declared righteous in the entirety of the Jewish Scriptures.

In this discussion I have had no intention of downplaying the abuse or injustices to women imposed upon them by the patriarchal society of that era. I have chosen, in accordance with the aims of this study, to emphasize how Tamar controlled her own destiny and how, in a sense, she stood patriarchy on its own head. My hope is that we can hold open multiple possibilities for reading this text, without assuming that only one reading may be properly drawn from it.

6

Some General Comments

The period of the lives of Abraham, Isaac, and Jacob is commonly referred to as the age of the patriarchs. The word "patriarch" literally means, "rule of the father." Based on the evidence presented thus far, one could possibly make a good case for calling it the age of the matriarchs, especially if one reads the stories from the viewpoint of the aforementioned idea of "hermeneutics of suspicion" that was popularized by Elizabeth Schussler Fiorenza[1] and regularly used by most feminist writers who came after her. This term simply means looking at the Biblical texts with the suspicion that the male authors of these texts may have deliberately suppressed or downplayed the roles of female characters in the story.[2] This could mean that Sarah, Rebekah, and the wives of Jacob exerted far more control than what we can glean from the texts. If this should appear as a denial of divine inspiration of the Bible, I would suggest precisely the opposite. That not every Biblical text equally reflects the nature of God is so obvious to any student of the Bible as to require no defense. I would suggest that we find clearest evidence of divine inspiration precisely in those texts that go against the grain of current customs and beliefs.[3] For the present thesis this would mean that the inspiration of God is to be seen most clearly when women are depicted as carrying out roles that would normally be reserved for men. As Tillman has put it, "It is ironic that the minority perspective in the Bible is usually the one where God is moving."[4] This assumption will underlie all that I write. Obviously, any-

---

1. Fiorenza, *In Memory of Her*, xxiii. See also Exum, *Fragmented Women*, 11–14.

2. I will later demonstrate one clear-cut example where an attempt has been made to suppress the role of one of the female daughters of Ephraim.

3. Cf. Scanzoni and Hardesty, *All We're Meant to Be*, 72.

4. Tillman, "Southern Baptists and Women in Ministry," 13.

one is free to accept or reject my assumption, but I wanted to spell it out clearly before proceeding further.

7

Zipporah

THE STORY OF ZIPPORAH is, rather characteristically, told in just a few verses in the book of Exodus. The earliest reference to her is in the second chapter of Exodus, where she becomes the wife of Moses. This happens during the period of Moses's flight from Egypt, necessitated by his killing an Egyptian who was abusing a fellow Hebrew slave (Exod 2:11–12). Moses fled to the land of Midian, where he encountered a priest of Midian who is here called Reuel (Exod 2:18). For an unspecified period of time Moses dwelt with Reuel,[1] and the latter gave his daughter Zipporah to Moses for a wife. To her were born two sons Gerhsom ("stranger") and Eliezer ("God is my help") [Exod 18:3–4].

We are not told what god Reuel served as a priest. Some have suggested that he was a priest to Yahweh,[2] and that Moses learned his Yahwistic faith from his father-in-law. I am not aware of anyone who has come up with a definitive answer to this issue and will leave it aside at this point.

As Moses was pasturing the flocks of his father-in-law (whatever his name may have been!), he encountered God at the burning bush and was commissioned to go back to Egypt and lead his fellow Hebrews out of

---

1. The name of Moses's father-in-law is a matter of considerable uncertainty. He is called Reuel in the passage mentioned above and in Numbers 10:29. The latter passage indicates that Hobab was the son of Reuel. Judges 4:11, however, identifies Hobab as the father-in-law of Moses. In Exodus 31 and in 18:5–12 Jethro is Moses's father-in-law. Perhaps we are dealing with a clan name and a family name, but we can only speculate regarding this. (cf. *The International Standard Bible Encyclopaedia*, s.v. "Reuel.")

2. In the unpointed Hebrew text of the Old Testament the personal name of God is Y(J)HWH. This name was considered to be too holy to be pronounced by human beings. Thus when vowel sounds came to be written in the Hebrew language, no one knew what vowels to insert, since the name had never been pronounced. Yahweh is an "educated guess" as to how the name should be pronounced. Another approach was to take the vowels from the word for "lord" and insert them into the name, yielding the hybrid form "Jehovah."

slavery. After an extended dialogue with God (Exod 3:10—4:17), Moses reluctantly accepted the commission, with Aaron as his mouthpiece (Exod 4:16). On the way to Egypt Zipporah again comes into the picture. Here we encounter one of the strangest passages in the Jewish Scriptures. It is a brief, self-contained unit in Exodus 2:24–26. At an unnamed lodging place on the way to Egypt, Yahweh sought to kill Moses, according to this text. At this point Zipporah took control of the situation and acted decisively. Apparently Zipporah (and Moses?) understood that the reason Yahweh wanted to kill Moses was that their son Gershom, and perhaps Moses himself, had not been circumcised in accordance with the covenant with Abraham (cf. Gen 17:12). Zipporah then took a flint knife and circumcised Gershom. She then threw the foreskin of Gershom at Moses's feet (or "touched his feet with it," which is another possible translation) and seemed to show a revulsion to the action she had just performed, if one accepts any of the translations mentioned below. The Hebrew text of what she said to Moses is relatively straightforward, but very difficult to interpret. According to the NASB her words are, "You are indeed a bridegroom of blood to me." In similar fashion the ASV and RSV read, "Surely a bridegroom of blood art thou to me." The KJV renders the same text (Exod 4:25), "Surely a bloody husband *art* thou to me." The NIV reads, "Surely you are a bridegroom of blood to me." The Douai-Rheims Version reads, "A bloody spouse art thou to me."

Another approach would put the above statement in an entirely different light. The word "feet" is a well-known ancient euphemism in the Jewish Scriptures for the sexual organs. One Biblical example of this euphemism is found in Isaiah 7:20.[3] In light of this fact, if one accepts the translation "touched his feet" regarding Zipporah's act, this could mean that by touching Moses's genitals with the foreskin, she had circumcised Moses by proxy. One other detail is necessary to interpret the reference to a "bridegroom of blood." Circumcision is known to have been a fairly widely practiced rite in preparation for marriage. Therefore the comment, "You are a bridegroom of blood to me" could have been a part of this ancient ritual being quoted by Zipporah. This only scratches the surface of possible interpretations of this brief passage.[4]

---

3. Although English translations sometimes obscure this fact, both the Hebrew and Greek text of Isaiah have the phrase "hair of the feet" at this point. One can scarcely interpret this in a literal fashion! See also Nunnally-Cox, *Foremothers*, 31.

4. For anyone who desires to pursue the matter further see Hubbard and Barker, gen.

Zipporah

What are we to make of the entire passage? It falls in what is generally considered to be the oldest strand of Hebrew tradition, the "J" or "Yahwist" strand, which took shape during the consolidation of the Hebrew monarchy under David and Solomon.[5] We should therefore expect to find a somewhat primitive, undeveloped, concept of God. This is how I would classify the idea that Yahweh wanted to kill Moses. As Honeycutt has commented, "One is hardly justified in concluding that Yahweh actually attempted to take the life of Moses."[6] Be that as it may, in the mind of the author of Exodus, Yahweh wanted to kill Moses; apparently because of his failure to circumcise Gershom. Further, Zipporah's decisive action saved Moses's life after he had somehow been rendered inactive. Lest one miss the obvious here, Zipporah performed a *priestly* act that was later not only prohibited for women, but for all men except those who belonged to the tribe of Levi.[7] As Bellis comments, "What is important is that Zipporah performs the ritual action, which later is done only by male priests. By her action, she saves Moses from God's wrath."[8] Cross takes the matter one step further, saying, "The priest of Midian provided Moses with a wife, apparently a priestess in her own right."[9]

---

eds., *Exodus*, 56–59; Clifton J. Allen, gen. ed., "Exodus," 336–37; Brenner, *The Israelite Woman*, 71–72.

5. Cf. Niditch, *Oral World and Written Word*, 110–14; John Carmody et. al., *Exploring the Hebrew Bible*, 15–17: and the chart in Anderson, *Understanding the Old Testament*, 453.

6. Allen, gen. ed., "Exodus," 337.

7. Cf. Parales, *Hidden Voices*, 22; Grits, *Paul, Women Teachers, and the Mother Goddess at Ephesus*, 63.

8. Bellis, *Helpmates Harlots Heroes*, 104.

9. Cross, *From Epic to Canon*, 61.

8

Shiphrah and Puah

SHIPHRAH AND PUAH ARE recorded in Exodus 1:8–22 in the account of the Israelites' slavery in Egypt as midwives who attended the birth of the Hebrew children. The reigning Pharaoh had come to fear the rapid multiplication of the Hebrews, and began to take increasingly severe measures to slow down their increase. His most drastic measure was to order all the male Hebrew babies to be killed. Shiphrah and Puah were to see that this was carried out. But, according to the Biblical author, these two midwives feared God and allowed the male babies to live, in direct opposition to the king's command (Exod 1:17). The king promptly called them in and asked why his command had been disobeyed. The story takes an amusing twist at this point. The two midwives play on the theme of racial/ethnic differences and tell the king that the Hebrew women are not like the Egyptian women—they gave birth so fast that the midwives could not get to them until the birth was already accomplished.

This is a brief story, but one that had a powerful impact on the future development of the Hebrew people. We can only imagine what the result would have been had not these two brave women had the courage to disobey the order of the most powerful man in their land. Bar-Ilan sums it up nicely: "Thus . . . the story of the midwives, Shiphrah and Puah, is an account of brave women who not only dared to transgress against the king's decree, but also had the effrontery to lie to him, endangering their own lives to save the lives of infants."[1] The story of the Hebrew people without Moses would have been drastically altered.

---

1. Bar-Ilan, *Some Jewish Women*, 2.

9

Miriam

CHRONOLOGICALLY THE STORY OF Miriam closely follows the story of Zipporah in the period the Israelites spent in the wilderness after their being delivered from Egyptian slavery under the leadership of Moses. During this period Moses was clearly the primary leader, according to the Biblical story, but his brother Aaron and his sister Miriam also played significant roles. Miriam received the title of female prophet (*nabiah*), a term rarely found in the Old Testament. As Bellis has noted, "Indeed, she is the first person—not the first woman, but the first person—in the Hebrew Bible given this title in its general sense."[1] Only four other women are ever given this title in the entirety of the Jewish Scriptures: Deborah (Judg 4:4), Huldah (2 Kgs 22:14; 2 Chr 34:22), Noadiah (Neh 6:14)[2], and the (unnamed) wife of the prophet Isaiah (Isa 8:3).[3] Rabbinical literature adds two other names, Abigail and Esther, to the list of women prophets.[4]

On one occasion Miriam joined with Aaron in challenging the supreme authority of Moses (Num 12:1–2). A parenthetical comment in this passage suggests that the real issue was a Cushite (Ethiopian) woman that Moses had married. Whether this woman is to be equated with Zipporah (mentioned as Moses's wife in Exod 2:21) or not is impossible to determine.[5] We may be seeing a very early occasion of racial or ethnic preju-

---

1. Bellis, *Helpmates Harlots Heroes*, 102.

2. In the Greek version of the Jewish Scriptures "Noadiah" has been changed to "Noadias," the masculine form of the name. This probably represents another case of male bias against the idea that a woman could fulfill the role of prophet.

3. Some try to interpret the term in the latter case as referring to the wife of the prophet, rather than she herself being a female prophet. See, e.g., Hubbard and Barker, eds., *Isaiah 1–33*, 133.

4. See Warren, "A Woman's Work," 7.

5. See discussion of John J. Owens in Allen, ed., *Leviticus-Ruth*, 118–19. Cf. Hubbard and Barker, eds., *Numbers*, 136, 138; Bellis, *Helpmates Harlots Heroes*, 102–6.

dice in this story. Be that as it may, Aaron and Miriam confronted Moses with the claim that God had spoken through them as well as Moses (Num 12:2). The three are then invited to a "summit meeting" by the Lord and are informed that God spoke uniquely to Moses (Num 12:4–8). Then we are told that the anger of the Lord burned against them (Aaron and Miriam) (Num 12:9). Inexplicably, this resulted in Miriam's being punished with leprosy, while Aaron got off scot-free (Num 12:10–15). As Elizabeth Cady Stanton commented more than a century ago, "As women are supposed to have no character or sacred office, it is always safe to punish them to the full extent of the law. So Miriam was not only afflicted with leprosy, but also shut out of the camp for seven days."[6] A "hermeneutics of suspicion" once more may be in order here. Some have tried to explain away the injustice by arguing that Aaron could not be given leprosy because this would have made him unclean and unable to carry out his priestly function. Others have suggested that two originally independent stories have been brought together here. Still others have pointed to the listing of Miriam's name first in the challenge to Moses and inferred from this that she was the primary instigator of the challenge.[7] Sakenfield puts the matter succinctly: "Despite these theories, the reality remains that in this story a woman and a man together commit the same sin, but the woman is punished and the man is not."[8]

There is yet at least one other reason for suspecting that we are not getting the full story in the passages discussed above. God, at a later point in Israel's history, spoke through the prophet Micah, "Indeed I brought you up from the land of Egypt and ransomed you from the house of slavery, and I sent before you Moses, Aaron and Miriam" (Micah 6:4).[9] This should erase any doubt that Miriam did in fact carry out a leadership function during the time the Israelites were in the wilderness. Hull points out that not only was Miriam a leader, but that she performed this leadership as a *single* woman.[10] This is not to suggest that Moses, Aaron, and Miriam were all on the same level in terms of their leadership.

---

6. Cited in Nunnally-Cox, *Foremothers*, 36.
7. See, for example, Grenz, *Women in the Church*, 68.
8. *Eerdmans Dictionary of the Bible*, s.v. "Miriam."
9. Cf. Bushnell, *God's Word to Women*, 95:780.
10. Hull, *Equal to Serve*, 113.

Miriam

To suggest this would be to claim too much; not to recognize that all three were placed in roles of leadership would be to claim too little.

One recent scholar has gone so far as to say that Miriam may have carried out some of the functions of priesthood. The same scholar aptly notes, "Without Miriam, there would not have been a Moses to confront Pharaoh and to lead the Hebrew people out of Egypt. Miriam is Moses's origin. This act of faith by a pious woman in her youth must not go unnoticed or unaccepted in our traditions."[11]

The text discussed above is the latest reference to Miriam in canonical Scripture. It is *not* the latest in Jewish tradition. In a tradition stemming from the first century CE known as *Pseudo-Philo*, Miriam is given credit for predicting the birth of Moses through a dream, among other things.[12] The same tradition states that God gave the Israelites the well at Marah because of Miriam, the pillar of cloud for Aaron, and the manna on account of Moses.[13] Although we can only guess as to the authenticity of this tradition, it strongly supports the joint leadership of Moses, Aaron, and Miriam.

---

11. Berquist, *Reclaiming Her Story*, 3, 80. For a rhetorical-critical approach which yields the reading that the story of Miriam has been largely squelched, see Murphy, *The Word according to Eve*, 55–59.

12. See discussion in Brown, *No Longer Be Silent*, 16–18.

13. Cited in Levine, ed., *Women Like This*, 93.

10

Mahlah, Noah, Hoglah, Milcah, and Tirzah

I suspect that the names of Mahlah, Noah, Hoglah, Milcah, and Tirzah look rather strange to most people—even to those who read the Bible a great deal. They are the daughters of one Zelophehad of the tribe of Manasseh. Zelophehad died without any sons (Num 27:3). By the rules of inheritance that prevailed at the time, only sons could inherit family property. These five women challenged those rules, arguing, "Why should the name of our father be withdrawn from among his family because he had no sons? Give us a possession among our father's brothers" (Num 27:4). (Note that both perpetuating the family name *and* the right to inherit property are involved here.) Moses listened to these sisters and presented their case to the Lord, who told Moses that they were right (Num 27:7). "This is possibly the only instance where the Lord, in the mind of the narrator, sides with a woman."[1] The efforts of these five sisters brought about fundamental changes in the laws of inheritance, permitting daughters the right to inherit property. To be sure, precedence was still given to sons; but at least in cases where there were no sons, daughters could now inherit family property.

Because Moses was not allowed to enter the land of Canaan, the actual allotment of the land fell to his successor Joshua. From Joshua 17:1–5 we learn that these same sisters successfully reasserted their rights before Joshua and Eleazer the priest. Apparently Mahlah, Noah, Hoglah, Milcah, and Tirzah were allotted an area of land in the same proportion as if they had been sons.

---

1. Nunnally-Cox, *Foremothers*, 39.

11

Rahab

Like many Biblical stories, the story of Rahab is told with considerable scarcity of detail. It is recorded in Joshua 1:1–21 and 6:22–25. The Israelites were about to embark upon the conquest of the land of Canaan, which they understood as being promised to them as a part of God's covenant with Abraham. As they moved westward across the Jordan River, the first obstacle to the conquest was the city-state of Jericho.[1]

As the story has been passed down, Joshua sent two young men as spies to gather information about the land, especially the area of Jericho (Josh 2:1a). They came into Jericho to the house of a prostitute named Rahab and lodged there (Josh 2:1b). Doubtless this was a daily occurrence that in and of itself would not have aroused any suspicion. In ways that we are not told, however, someone recognized the two young men as Israelites who had come to spy out the land and reported this information to the king of Jericho (Josh 2:2). Upon hearing this, he went to the house of Rahab and ordered her to bring out the two men, informing her of their intent to spy out the land (Josh 2:3). Rahab admitted that two men had come into her house, but denied knowing where they were from. She further (falsely) informed him that the two men had left just before the time of the shutting of the city gates, and that if he moved quickly he could overtake them. Her story was so believable, in that men would usually have stayed at Rahab's house for only brief periods of time, that the king's representatives neither questioned her story nor searched her house. She had in fact hidden the two men under stalks of flax upon her roof (Josh 2:4–7).

---

1. There was no central government in the land of Canaan. The land was dotted with city-states modeled after the Greek *polis*. Petty kings controlled each city-state and the immediately surrounding territory.

As soon as the messengers of the king departed on their "wild goose chase," Rahab went up on the roof and discussed the fate of her land with the two Israelite spies. She told them that word of the Israelites' deliverance from Egypt was well known and acknowledged that the Lord had given her land to the Israelites. She even went so far as to make a confession of faith in the Israelites' God (Josh 2:8–11). She then extracted a promise from the spies that they would spare her life and the lives of her family when they conquered the land. They made a solemn promise to do this and swore her to secrecy on this promise. There were, however, two conditions to their promise. The first was that Rahab would have her entire family in her house with her. The second was that she would tie a scarlet cord in the window so that her house could easily be identified by the approaching Israelites (Josh 2:17–19). She then let the spies down from her window by a rope, advising them to go into the hills and wait three days for the men who were searching for them to give up (Josh 2:15–16). (Rahab's house was probably built into the wall of Jericho itself, so the spies as they were let down from her window would have then been outside the city. Excavations in the twentieth century have revealed an inner wall of Jericho that was 12 to 15 feet thick and an outer wall about 6 feet thick and which "probably rose originally to 25 or 30 feet."[2])

The Israelite spies followed Rahab's advice and then returned to their people. As Rendsberg has aptly noted, "Throughout the episode, Rahab has the upper hand—she is wiser and more resourceful than all the other characters in the story, including the Israelite spies . . . Furthermore, so ignoble are the spies that we never even learn their names."[3] Winters well describes Rahab in these words: "Cunning, quick-witted, and assertive, Rahab bargained with spies, lied to soldiers, and took charge of her own life. She was unmarried and quite capable of looking after herself."[4]

The final glimpse we get of Rahab comes with the capture of Jericho by Joshua and the Israelites. Joshua understood God as saying that the entire city was to be put "under the ban," which meant destroying every living human or animal in the city, then burning it with fire. The only exception to this destruction was that everything made of gold, silver,

---

2. *Black's Bible Dictionary*, s.v. "Jericho."
3. Rendsburg, *Unlikely Heroes*, 19–20.
4. Winters, *Rahab*.

bronze, or iron was to be placed in the "house" of the Lord.[5] Before burning the city, Joshua sent the two spies to Rahab's house and brought her family and their possessions outside the city (Josh 6:22–23). The Biblical narrator then informs us that because she hid the messengers of Joshua she and her family lived among Israel "to this day" (Josh 6:25).

This concludes the story of Rahab as we have it in the Jewish Scriptures. The appearance of her name in the Christian Testament, however, suggests that we do not have anywhere near the complete story. Her name appears at three points in the Christian Testament. The first appearance is in the genealogy of Jesus (Matt 1:5). Next, she is included in the long list of past heroes of faith (Heb 11:31). Finally she is presented, along with Abraham, as one who was justified by a faith that led to action (James 2:21–25).

The esteem shown for Rahab in the Christian Testament has been a problem for both Jews and Christians. She was not only in the lineage of Jesus of Nazareth, but also of the great King David. Hence many arguments have been devised to argue that Rahab was not really a prostitute. By the time of the Jewish historian Josephus (first century CE) Rahab has been transformed into an innkeeper.[6] (Although from what is known about inns during this period of time, one could question whether or not this really changes her status as a prostitute.) As one reads the various arguments that attempt to change Rahab's status into something more respectable, they basically conclude that "prostitute" in the Biblical text doesn't really mean prostitute! I would suggest that we simply accept the fact that Rahab was engaged in a dishonorable profession but, like any other sinner, she could become a person of faith and be used by God in a great way. In the words of Norah Lofts, "The meditations and searchings of centuries leave only one thing certain about her—her profession."[7]

In light of this discussion, perhaps a word needs to be said about the attitude toward prostitutes and prostitution in ancient Israel. No uniform position can be found on the subject in the Jewish Scriptures. As noted above, Judah was not faulted by the Biblical writer for going to a woman he assumed to be a prostitute. On the other hand, the law forbade

---

5. This would have meant the tabernacle, or tent, that the Israelites had been instructed to make during their time in the wilderness. The first temple was not built until a couple of centuries later during the kingship of Solomon.

6. *Antiquities* v.i.ii.

7. Lofts, *Women in the Old Testament*, 56.

a priest to marry a prostitute (Lev 21:7, 14). (The fact that only priests are specified might suggest that no such prohibition was placed on other Israelites.) Furthermore, the hire of either female or male prostitutes was not to be brought into the "house" of the Lord for a votive offering (Deut 23:18).[8] Also, one was not to force a daughter into prostitution because this would "profane" her (Lev 19:29).

In the light of these passages, and hints gleaned here and there in the Jewish Scriptures, perhaps the best we can do is suggest that prostitution was tolerated but never looked upon favorably for the most part.[9] Bellis has summarized the attitude toward prostitution in ancient Israel perhaps as well as any: "In Hebrew society, harlots were outcasts who were tolerated but not held in honor."[10]

Some would perhaps question why I would include Rahab as a woman who did not fit into the patriarchal mold for a woman. She was not even an Israelite. She was a "woman of ill repute." I will argue that she was also a woman of independence, faith, and resolve who refused to accept the position allotted to women in her society; and who cast a long shadow of influence over the people of God in the Jewish Scriptures.

First of all, as we go back to the story itself, we note that she was self-sufficient. She was not under the control or authority of any male. This of itself sets her apart. And, as Berquist has noted, her independence would have separated her from her society more than her sexual activities.[11]

Second, no one can read this story without seeing that Rahab demonstrated tremendous courage—something considered to be a manly virtue in her world. As Brenner puts it, "Rahab was in danger of being exposed as a traitor to her home town."[12] Had the representatives of the king of Jericho not taken her word, and searched her house, she could very well have been executed as a traitor.

Third, I would point out that she negotiated with the (male) Hebrew spies from a position of strength. She could very easily have turned them over to the king of Jericho, in which case they would probably have been tortured in an attempt to gain information about the planned conquest

---

8. It is generally accepted among scholars that "dog" in this passage refers to a male prostitute, rather than to a four-legged animal.

9. For further discussion, see Bar-Ilan, *Some Jewish Women*, 132–55.

10. Bellis, *Helpmates Harlots Heroes*, 13.

11. Berquist, *Reclaiming Her Story*, 83.

12. Brenner, *The Israelite Woman*, 119.

Rahab

by the Israelites—and probably killed in the end. Rahab did not hesitate to say, in effect, "You owe me one now—and I have every intention of collecting!" (cf. Josh 2:12–13). Although the language of Joshua 2:12 admittedly seems like an entreaty, Rahab is obviously saying that, because she had shown *chesed* ("kindness," "mercy") to them, they should show *chesed* to her and her family—and the unspoken part of the exchange was that they were still in her power. She could choose at any point to turn them over to the local authorities.

Finally, I would return to the faith of Rahab. If we restricted our attention to the story in the Hebrew Bible, we might reasonably question the genuineness of her proclamation of faith in the God of the Israelites. Obviously she and her people were in a very difficult position, and so her confession could be read as simply an attempt to save her life and that of her people, a sort of "foxhole theology."[13] However, this is not the way her story was read by future generations. Evidence for this has been presented above in her placement in the genealogy of Jesus and her being listed among prominent persons of faith in Hebrews and James.

---

13. For those of the younger generation who may not understand this sort of language, during World War II it was widely acclaimed that there were no atheists to be found in foxholes. When it came to matters of life and death, everyone believed in God.

12

Achsah

Once more we encounter a name not widely known and that finds its way into Scripture in a very brief, sketchy fashion. Achsah is mentioned as a daughter of Caleb in 1 Chronicles 2:49. Somewhat parallel accounts of her story also appear in Joshua 15:16–19 and Judges 1:12–15. The setting is in the story of the Israelite conquest of Canaan. Caleb, the first judge of Israel, offered to give his daughter as a wife to whoever would capture the city of Debir. Caleb's nephew Othniel took the challenge, captured the city, and received Achsah as his wife. Thus far we seem to have a woman who, in traditional fashion, was totally subject to the males in her life. But how much of the story are we missing? Clearly both accounts assume that Caleb has given his daughter lands in the arid south country, although there is no mention of it in either of the texts mentioned above. Further, at the point where Achsah comes to Othniel we find some very interesting textual variations. The Greek text of the passage from Joshua reads, "She counseled with him, saying, I will ask my father for a field" (Josh 15:18b). The Greek text of the passage from Judges reads, "And as she came to him (Othniel, her new husband), *he* persuaded *her* to ask for a field from her father" (Judges 1:14a) (emphasis mine). What makes this the more interesting is that in the Hebrew text of both passages some of the manuscripts contain this reading. Edward Dalglish, whom I know personally as a very meticulous Hebrew scholar, asserts without question that the proper reading in Judges 1:14 is the one in which Othniel persuades Achsah to ask for a field from her father.[1]

Once more it appears that we have evidence in the ancient texts of an attempt to "tame" a woman who may have become too self-assertive for the good of the patriarchal system of her day. Given the prevailing

---

1. Allen, gen. ed., "Judges," 392 n. 10.

evidence that Othniel persuaded her to ask for a field from her father, we might entertain the question as to *why* he did so. After all, to ask for a dowry from the father of the bride was an ancient and honored tradition. For Othniel to have asked for himself would have been completely acceptable. I would raise the possibility that Othniel persuaded Achsah to make this request because she was the stronger personality and would have a better chance of success. In favor of this understanding, note the brevity of Achsah's request and Caleb's granting that request. To paraphrase, she said to him, "You have given me all this dry, desert land—now give me some water to go with it—and he gave her the upper and lower springs" (or perhaps cisterns—translation of the Hebrew text is uncertain at this point). Her request is granted without any question or discussion, according to the Biblical text. Whether my speculation goes too far, I will leave the reader to judge. Any way we may interpret the text, however, this much seems clear: although she seems to have accepted her father's right to give her to a man as a wife, Achsah did not blindly submit to whatever her father and/or her husband chose to give her. I would suggest that this is quite remarkable for the era in which she lived.

13

Deborah

ONE OF THE MOST remarkable stories of female leadership in the Hebrew Bible is that of Deborah. She is described as both a prophetess and a judge in Israel (Judg 4:4). In the Jewish Scriptures we find side by side both a prose account and a poetic account of her time as judge. These accounts are found in Judges 4 and 5 respectively. Both accounts contain numerous similarities, as well as significant differences of detail. The differences include, but are not limited to, the following: (1) The prose account suggests that only the tribes of Zebulun and Naphthali took part in the battle against Jabin and his military commander Sisera, whereas the poetic account adds the tribes of Ephraim, Benjamin, Issachar, and Reuben (Judg 5:14–15). (2) The prose account describes a more or less traditional battle in which the Israelite forces totally annihilated the forces under Sisera (Judg 4:14–16), whereas the poetic account suggests a violent storm, which rendered Sisera's chariots ineffective; and a swollen brook Kishon that swept the Canaanite armies away (Judg 5:21). (The Jewish historian, Flavius Josephus, supports the poetic account: "So the battle began; and when they were come to close fight, there came down from heaven a great storm, with a vast quantity of rain and hail, and the wind blew the rain in the face of the Canaanites, and so darkened their eyes, that their arrows and slings were of no advantage to them, nor would the coldness of the air permit the soldiers to make use of their swords; while this storm did not so much incommode the Israelites, because it came in their backs."[1]) (3) The prose account locates the battle at the "river" Kishon (Judg 4:7), whereas the poetic account gives the position as near Taanach (Judg 5:19). (The latter, however, was located close enough to the brook Kishon that the difference may be merely a different choice of

---

1. *Antiquities*, v.v.iv.

ways to specify the location of the battle.) (4) The prose account omits the significant title for Deborah, "Mother in Israel," which the poetic account contains (Judg 5:7). (5) There are several differences, some of which are subtle, between the two accounts of Sisera's death at the hand of Jael the Kenite. The prose account presents a picture of Sisera going to sleep after receiving milk from Jael and the latter driving a tent peg through his head while he is asleep (Judg 4:21). It says nothing of his falling in any way. The poetic account, on the other hand, does not have the detail that Sisera was asleep, and says he fell *between the feet* of Jael (Judg 5:26–27). Obviously this does not harmonize well with the detail in the prose account that Sisera was asleep when Jael struck him. Some have seen in this detail evidence of a sexual encounter, or attempt thereat, on the part of Sisera.[2] I will return to the story of Jael later.

Most scholars suggest that the poetic version of the story of Deborah is older than the prose version. If this be correct, Deborah's status is considerably enhanced by the title "Mother in Israel" in the older version. As Carol Meyers has aptly noted, "Deborah—is called 'mother in Israel' (Judg 5:7). The designation 'mother' does not refer to a biological maternal role (we actually know nothing about her family except for her husband's name) but rather to her divinatory leadership. Like 'father,' 'mother' sometimes was a title for someone bearing a particular kind of religious authority."[3]

According to Judges 4 Deborah had a male counterpart named Barak. Deborah summoned him to her, announcing that God had commanded an army to march against the oppressing Canaanite army led by Sisera. She further informed Barak that God had promised to deliver Sisera into his hand (Judg 4:7). Astoundingly, Barak answered, "If you will go with me, then I will go; but if you will not go with me, I shall not go" (Judg 4:8). No unusual intelligence is required to see that the real leader of the Israelites at this point was the woman Deborah; not Barak or any other male. She *summoned* Barak—and he not only came but openly capitulated to her leadership. Furthermore, there is not even a hint in the text that this was considered either improper or extraordinary. In Schmidt's words, "Deborah was neither silent nor submissive, and she acted as God's

2. This is hinted somewhat in Pseudo-Philo's *Biblical Antiquities* 31:3. For an extended discussion of the portrait of Deborah in this work, see Cheryl Brown, *No Longer Silent*, 40–71.

3. Meyers, *Discovering Eve*, 159–60.

mouthpiece. These three activities have been conveniently overlooked by many theologians."[4]

Grady has noted the pervasive tendency among conservative theologians to cast Barak as a weakling who needed a "mother figure" to go into battle with him. He notes that Barak is listed in the "roll call of the faithful" in Hebrews 11, without any hint that he was lacking in manliness. Grady goes on to say, "He was a man's man—most likely a brave general. But he knew that Israel had no chance to win this war against the superior armies of the Canaanites unless God performed a military miracle. Barak did, in fact, expect that miracle, but he knew it would not happen unless God's appointed prophet went along. That is why he wanted Deborah by his side. It had nothing to do with her gender. He knew that only God's power could defeat a hostile army equipped with nine hundred iron chariots."[5]

A "hermeneutics of suspicion" would lead us to question how many similar stories of women in that era may have been suppressed. The fact that we have even one such remarkable story of a woman's leadership is, in my judgment, an indicator of divine inspiration.

Needless to say, those who would propagate patriarchy[6] have spared no effort in attempting to discredit or minimize the obvious implications of this story. One approach has been to basically disregard the story, because this is the only hint of any judge in the Jewish Scriptures who was not male. As noted in the paragraph above, I would draw the exact opposite conclusion.

Another approach is the rather tired old argument that Deborah had to step in because no man made himself available to meet the challenge. As Groothuis has noted, "John Piper and Wayne Grudem believe that Deborah's leadership actually affirmed 'the usual leadership of men' by serving as a rebuke to the men of Israel who should have had the courage to take on leadership of the nation themselves."[7] If that were the case,

---

4. Alvin John Schmidt, *Veiled and Silenced*, 148.

5. Grady, *25 Tough Questions about Women*, 110–11.

6. I am using this term in a fairly loose fashion to denote those who take the position that males are assigned all leadership functions in all areas of life, and females are to submit to the leadership of males. For a technical discussion of the meaning of patriarchy I refer the reader to the excellent discussion in Meyers, *Discovering Eve*, 24–46.

7. Rebecca Groothuis, *Good News for Women*, 190. Cf. also Grady, *Tough Questions about Women*, 110.

one wonders why nothing whatever in the text says, or even implies, that Deborah was chosen because no man volunteered.

Another attempt to "tame" Deborah and place her in a more traditional role has been a (highly questionable) claim that she was in fact married. Where the text describes Deborah as "the woman of Lappidoth" (Judg 4:4), those who take this position argue that "Lappidoth" is a man's name and that Deborah was his wife. However, the word "lappidoth" means something like "a spirited woman," making it highly unlikely to have been the name of a man. Although the Hebrew lends itself to this possible translation (as the name of a man), no further support can be found in the text. There is no evidence in the Bible of a man named Lappidoth aside from treating the word in Judges 4:4 as the name of a man. Brenner probably exposes the true motivation of those who argue that Deborah was married when she comments, "The Jewish Sages, who speculated about Lappidoth, identified him with Barak, thus supplying Deborah with 'wifely' integrity and womanhood. This interpretation . . . is informed by the extralinguistic opinion that a woman, even when she is active in the public sphere, should retain her distinctive duties and sexuality."[8]

Yet another tactic by traditionalists is to argue that Deborah's prophetic leadership of Israel was less authoritative than that of men. They argue that Deborah did not prophesy in public—people came to her in private for a word from the Lord, and it is not said that the Lord raised up Deborah as is said of the male judges. Thomas Schreiner represents this position, saying that Deborah's rule "was different from that of the other judges in that she did not exercise leadership over men."[9] Such an argument is rather ludicrous, and Groothuis refutes it by pointing out that, "Although she did not lead the men into battle herself, she directed the man who did."[10]

Stanley Grenz aptly observes that "Schreiner's concern to harmonize the account with his male headship principle is foreign to the concern of the biblical author. Deborah commanded Barak to assemble the army.

---

8. Brenner, *The Israelite Woman*, 120.
9. Cited in Rebecca Groothuis, *Good News for Women*, 191.
10. Ibid.

To suggest that this does not entail the exercise of authority over a man in an official capacity presses the text into a procrustean bed."[11]

In view of the arguments discussed above that Deborah's judgeship was *different* from that of the male judges, it should only be fair to point out a major point of similarity. The poetic form of her story in Judges 5 has been previously noted, plus the scholarly opinion that this is the earlier of the two accounts. Admittedly, the poem is portrayed as the song of Deborah *and* Barak. I have already pointed out, however, how Barak openly capitulated to the leadership of Deborah. Furthermore, the reference to Deborah as a "Mother in Israel" (v. 7) may be seen as pointing to her higher leadership role. Immediately after the conclusion of the poem, one brief prose sentence is recorded: "And the land was undisturbed for forty years" (Judg 5:31b). The identical statement follows the story of the judgeship of Othniel (Judg 3:11), Ehud (Judg 3:30),[12] and that of Gideon (Judg 8:28).[13] All of this seems to suggest that the author of the book of Judges intended for us to place Deborah's judgeship, with Barak in a supporting role, on a par with any and all of her male counterparts. To deny that she exercised leadership and authority over any males is simply ludicrous, given the details in the biblical text itself. That text seems to lend full support to the summary statement by Sakenfeld: "In sum, despite the military context that may give us pause, Deborah may be seen as a model for women in authority in the religious sphere and as a model for cooperation between women and men."[14] Or, in Groothuis's words, "This is the

---

11. Grenz with Kjesbo, *Women in the Church*, 238 n. 10.

12. Except that the period of time is eighty years instead of forty. These numbers are in all probability symbolic, given the number of judges to whom a reign of forty years or a multiple thereof is assigned. (cf. Anderson, *Understanding the Old Testament*, 113.) If we take the numbers literally and add them all together, the number of years is approximately double the number of years the period of the judges lasted. Taking the general scholarly consensus that Rameses II was the pharaoh of the exodus, and the end of the period came with the reign of David around 1000 BCE, we are left with a little less than two hundred years for the period of the judges. If one dates the beginning of the monarchy with the reign of Saul, the number of years is reduced still further. I am aware that not all scholars agree that Rameses II was the pharaoh of the exodus, and there is further disagreement as to the years he reigned, but I think what I have suggested is a fairly general scholarly consensus.

13. Although the statement in Judges 3:11 reads "Then the land had rest forty years" in the NASB, ASV, KJV, RSV, and perhaps others, in both the Hebrew and Greek texts the statements are identical with those in Judges 3:30 and 8:28.

14. Sakenfeld, "Deborah, Jael and Sisera's Mother," 13–22.

Deborah

sort of position to which God called a woman—even before the new covenant in Christ did away with all spiritual distinctions between male and female! Deborah may have been the only female judge of Israel, but she was a judge, nonetheless, called by God to rule with both civil and spiritual authority. Those who wish to derogate the importance and authority of her rulership on account of her gender find no encouragement toward this end from the actual biblical text."[15] Christina Campbell has added her voice to this refrain in these words: "Deborah's prophet/judgeship was not a private little cottage industry being practiced out of her home. In view of the text there can be little doubt that Deborah was the recognized, appointed leader/judge of the Israelites at that time. I mention this fairly obvious fact only because of the persistent rejection or downplaying of Deborah's authority by traditional patriarchalists: Deborah does not fit into their male 'headship' theory of God's economy."[16] Parales has noted the parallels between Deborah and the great prophet Samuel: "Deborah had carried out the three functions that marked the ministry of Samuel: Judge over Israel, prophet, and commissioner of military leaders."[17]

A parting word about Deborah is that gender bias had already begun to assert itself by the time the Christian Testament came into being. In the Book of Hebrews, chapter eleven, we read a long list of those of the past who had lived a life of faith. Nunnally-Cox puts this in the mildest of terms, saying, "After reading the story of Deborah and Barak, it is a bit surprising to see Barak named among the judges, while Deborah is nowhere mentioned."[18] The surprise is only for those who are unacquainted with the deep-seated male bias of the Biblical writings.

---

15. Rebecca Groothuis, *Good News for Women*, 192.
16. Cited in Grenz with Muirkjesbo, *Women in the Church*, 69–70.
17. Parales, *Hidden Voices*, 22.
18. Nunnally-Cox, *Foremothers*, 50; cf. Heb 11:32.

14

Jael

Some details of Jael's life somewhat overlap the story of Deborah and have been discussed above. The differences between the prose account in Judges 4 and the poetic account in Judges 5 have been noted. In both accounts Jael is credited with the killing of the leader of the forces doing battle with the Israelites. In the mind of the Biblical author of the book of Judges, we are no doubt intended to see this as a fulfillment of Deborah's prediction that, since Barak had capitulated to her leadership, God would give the victory to a woman (Judg 4:8–9). Jael is highly lauded for her actions and seems to be placed upon the same level as the judges of Israel. In Judges 5:6–7 her name appears between that of Shamgar and Deborah. If this be a different Jael than the one praised in Judges 5:24–27 there is no evidence of that, either within the text or outside of it. The parallel lines "in the days of Shamgar" and "in the days of Jael" (Judg 5:6ab) strongly point to the idea that she was thought of as being on a par with the judges, even though she was a Kenite and not an Israelite. Later Jewish tradition clearly places her in the role of judge: "In the days when the judges judged, woe unto that generation which judges it [sic] judges, and woe unto the generation whose judges are in need of being judged! As it is said, 'And yet they harkened not unto their judges' (Jud. 2:12) [sic]. Who were (the judges in question)? Rab said; 'They were Barak and Deborah.' R. Joshua b. Levi said: 'They were Shamgar and Ehud.' R. Huna said: 'They were Deborah, Barak, and Jael.' The word 'judge' implies one, 'judges' implies two, 'the judges' three."[1] Although the text tells us that the Kenites were at peace with Jabin, king of Hazor (and Sisera's boss), at this point (Judg 4:17), there was a more ancient tie between the Kenites

---

1. *Ruth Rabbah* 1:1 as cited in Caspi and Cohen, *Still Watters Run Deep*, 89.

Jael

and the Israelites, in that Moses's father-in-law Jethro (or Reuel or Raguel[2] or Hobab, or whatever his name may have been (see above) was a Kenite (Judg 4:11). This could have played a role in Jael's decision to cast her loyalty with the Israelites, although there is no direct evidence of this in the text.

Jael has often been faulted for violating the unwritten law of desert hospitality, which required the protection of a guest at any and all costs. Sakenfeld notes that such a charge is better substantiated by the prose version in Judges 4 than the poetic version of Judges 5. She further notes that a male visitor would normally have been received by a male, and that the reference to Jael's tent might indicate that Sisera was in a women's area that would normally be off limits to all males.[3] If Sakenfeld is on the right track here, we would be justified in suggesting that Sisera may have had rape on his mind, and that the normal rules of hospitality would not apply to this particular situation. Sakenfeld goes on to say with regard to Judges 5:27,

> Given that all these words in the verse are capable of double meaning in relation to sex and death, it seems reasonable to read the poem with this double meaning in view. Sisera, who in usual circumstances would be the potential rapist, the aggressor, the one who may kill when he is finished with the woman, is instead pictured in the role and posture of the woman who seeks with supplication and turning to ward off her rapist. Jael, who in usual circumstances would be the supplicant and victim, is pictured in the role and posture of initiator, victor, perhaps we must say aggressor. So although the poem taunts Sisera's people with the report of his death at the hands of a woman, it does so in a way that says "no" to rape in the context of war.[4]

Sakenfeld considerably heightens the discussion of the possibility that Sisera was bent upon rape when he entered the tent of Jael in these words:

> Whether or not Sisera entered restricted quarters, the poetic language used in describing his death is full of sexual overtones. The

---

2. The KJV and Douay-Rheims versions give this as the name of Moses's father-in law in Num 10:29. I am not aware of any other versions in which the name Raguel appears.
3. Sakenfeld, *Deborah, Jael and Sisera's Mother*, 13–22. See also Bellis, *Helpmates Harlots Heroes*, 119–23.
4. Ibid.

principal clue is the appearance of the word *feet* (NRSV; Hebrew *raglaim*) in 5:27. The NRSV translation pictures Sisera on the ground at Jael's feet (literally). But Hebrew certainly knows an alternative, euphemistic meaning of the word *feet* as genitals. And the Hebrew word also can mean *legs*. Hence Niditch, Wansbrough, and others translate *between her legs* (with clear sexual overtones) rather than *at her feet* (emphasis original). Niditch renders the key verse as follows:

> Between her legs he knelt, he fell, he lay
> Between her legs he knelt, he fell
> Where he knelt, there he fell, despoiled.

Niditch has shown that the vocabulary for kneeling (NRSV "sank"), lying (NRSV "lay still"), and despoiling (NRSV, "dead") all appear both in contexts of death and in sexual contexts, often of sexual betrayal.[5]

A still later Jewish tradition than the one mentioned above, known as *Pseudo-Philo*, probably dating from the first century CE, amplifies the story of Jael considerably. That writer comments that Jael was a very beautiful woman, and that she adorned herself before going out to meet him. Sisera is said to declare that if he is saved he will go to his mother and Jael will become his wife. Another added detail is that she sought a sign from the Lord that if, after waking up from sleep, Sisera would ask for water to drink she would know that killing him was the Lord's will. Furthermore, Jael not only gives Sisera milk to drink in this text, but wine mixed with milk. Sisera is also presented as being conscious enough after being struck by Jael to say he was dying like a woman. Jael then tells him to go and boast to his father in Hell that he had fallen into the hands of a woman![6]

Perhaps worth noting here is the fact that death at the hands of a woman was the most ignominious death imaginable in the ancient world (cf. the story of Abimelech in Judges 9:52–54). We are probably intended to see a major role reversal as well. As the song about Sisera's mother in Judges 4:28–30 indicates, Sisera was expected to capture Jewish maidens as a part of the spoils of war. Instead, the great conqueror of maidens himself became captive to a woman!

---

5. Ibid.

6. Charlesworth, ed., *The Old Testament Pseudepigrapha*, II:344–45. Cf. also discussion in Levine, ed., *Women Like This*, 101–4 and Cheryl Brown, *No Longer Be Silent*, 51–54.

Jael

As with Deborah, patriarchalists have attempted to deny the obvious; this time by claiming that Jael was a man. As Murphy has noted, "'Jael' was and is a well-known woman's name. Jael—the famous Jael who drives a tent peg through the head of Sisera—is prominent in Judges. But a number of contemporary scholars have hunted through Scripture and other ancient sources to see if they can find a precedent for a Jael who is a man, because it seems to them so unlikely that this Jael could have been a woman."[7] No such precedent has yet been found, and we are left with a Biblical story in which a woman slays an enemy general, a role which only men would have been expected to play in that day. Niditch provides an excellent summation of the picture of Jael: "Jael is a symbolization of self-assertion, a force of change, one who breaks free heroically from oppressive and suppressive forces. . . . The tale is rich in images of directed action, self assertion, and consciousness on the part of the underdog."[8]

---

7. Murphy, *The Word according to Eve*, 192.
8. Niditch, "Eroticism and Death in the Tale of Jael," 52–53.

15

Sheerah

SHEERAH IS A NAME that I suspect many, even those most familiar with the Bible, would not recognize. I found her tucked away in the genealogical section of 1 Chronicles—a safe hiding place in that very few people ever read the Biblical genealogies. First Chronicles contains a single verse in the genealogy of Ephraim that is mind-boggling in its ancient context. The verse reads as follows: "And his daughter was Sheerah, who built lower and upper Beth-horon, and also Uzzen-Sheerah (1 Chr 7:24)." Although the latter site has never been discovered, the two Beth-horons were prominent in Old Testament history. They controlled the easiest access from the Mediterranean coastal plain to the road linking Shechem and Jerusalem. The pass that these cities flanked was used by Philistine raiding parties in the time of Saul and by Pharaoh Shishak in the time of King Josiah; just to mention a couple of facts that highlight the strategic and military significance of the two Beth-horons.[1] The fact that 2 Chronicles 8:5 gives Solomon credit for founding these cities *may* indicate an attempt to refute the tradition that they were built by a woman. Some scholars have even questioned the authenticity of the passage on the basis that women just didn't build cities in those days. That tradition has been obscured in more than one way by modern scholars. I examined four Bible dictionaries without finding even a brief article on Sheerah. She was mentioned in the articles on Beth-horon and Uzzen-Sheerah, but was not given a separate entry. One scholar referred to these cities as being built by a *group* from Ephraim—although there is absolutely nothing in the text to indicate that the names represent groups rather than individuals.[2] As noted above, others have challenged the authentic-

---

1. *Mercer Dictionary of the Bible*, s.v. "Beth-horon."
2. *Black's Bible Dictionary*, s.v. "Sherah."

ity of the passage, although no textual evidence in either the Hebrew or Greek versions of the Jewish Scriptures supports this conclusion.[3] Clyde T. Francisco, a well-known Baptist scholar of another generation, cites Curtis and Madsen as advocating the position that the cities were built by a group from Ephraim, and then adds: "This is exactly the point of the account. Here is a woman doing something that only men had done before."[4]

Such evasions as I have mentioned above are already present in the Greek version of the Old Testament. There Uzzen-Sheerah has become one of the sons of Ephraim instead of a third city built by his daughter Sheerah. Sheerah's name is not mentioned at all, but a third person singular form of the verb "to build" is a telltale sign that the text has been tampered with. (In the Greek language, unlike anything in English with which we might be familiar, verbs were inflected to show the person and number of the subject.) In the Greek text as it stands there is no singular subject in this verse or the immediate context. I think there can be no reasonable doubt that the subject was Sheerah, just as the Hebrew text has it.

The image of a woman as a builder of cities was apparently too much for some to accept, by either ancient or modern interpreters, if the Hebrew text be taken at face value. Sheerah was obviously not a submissive woman. That she could build these cities without being in a position of authority over numerous male workers strains the bounds of possibility, to say the least.

---

3. Cf. *The International Standard Bible Encyclopaedia*, s.v. "Sheerah."
4. Allen, gen. ed., *1 Samuel-Nehemiah*, 320.

16

Ruth

However we may read the text of Ruth, it represents one of the more beautiful stories in the Bible. Some words of Ruth to her mother-in-law Naomi have been immortalized in the beautiful song, "Whither Thou Goest I Will Go." Most Americans are familiar with those words, whether or not they have any idea of their source. I will first give a brief summary of the story, then present some different readings of it. Recent feminist scholars have shown clearly that there is more to this story than meets the eye.

The setting of the story is specified in a very general way as the time when the judges ruled Israel. This would place it somewhere between 1200 and 1000 BCE. Scholars of the Jewish Scriptures are deeply divided as to the time of writing. Advocates can be found for dating the writing in the actual period of the judges, the period of the monarchy, and the time after the Jews returned from Babylonian captivity. A post-Biblical Jewish tradition has credited the prophet Samuel with the writing of Ruth, but the reliability of this tradition cannot be determined.[1] The placement of this book in the Hebrew canon of Scripture (in the third major division, between Proverbs and Song of Solomon) could be seen as suggesting that its writing belongs in the post-exilic period, as some recent scholars have suggested.[2] I will leave aside this question for now and focus on the story itself.

The story of Ruth revolves around Naomi ("my pleasantness") who, along with her husband and two sons, migrated into the land of Moab because of a severe famine in Judah. A brief look at the origin of the Moabites is in order at this point so that the story may be more fully ap-

---

1. Caspi & Cohen, *Still Waters Run Deep*, 89.
2. See, for example, Bellis, *Helpmates Harlots Heroes*, 208.

preciated. According to Genesis 20:30–38, the daughters of Lot, thinking their father was the only male not destroyed with Sodom and Gomorrah, decided that the only way for the family to continue was for them to have sexual relations with their father. Accordingly, they took turns in giving Lot wine to the point that he was unconscious of what was happening and seduced him. As a result, two sons were born who were named Moab and ben-Ammi. These became the progenitors of the Moabites and the Ammonites respectively; people who occupied the area east of the Jordan River when the Israelites came out from Egypt under the leadership of Moses. Because they stood in the way of the Israelites' conquest of the land, a mostly hostile relationship developed between them and the Israelites, a hostility that flared up at numerous points in the succeeding history of the Israelite people.[3] As LaCocque comments, "No one with the desire to shock his or her Israelite readership could have chosen a 'hero' more controversial, even repulsive, than a woman from Moab."[4]

To return to the story, after arriving in Moab, Naomi's two sons married local women named Ruth and Orpah. No sons were born from either of these marriages, and over a period of time Elimelech, Naomi's husband, and both her sons died. Naomi then decided to return to her native Judah. She encouraged her two daughters-in-law to go back to their own families and find other husbands. This was thought to be their only hope in the patriarchal society of which they were a part. Orpah returned home, but Ruth insisted upon coming to Judah with Naomi. This is where the words of the song mentioned above originated. Ruth not only vowed to go wherever Naomi went, but to claim both Naomi's god and people as her own. At this point Ruth becomes the central figure in the story. In order to provide food for herself and Naomi she goes out to glean in the barley fields during harvest time. She just "happened" to glean in the field of one Boaz, who just "happened" to be related to Naomi. As Trible comments, "It is a felicitous expression, 'she happened to come,' reporting chance and accident while hinting that chance is caused. Within human luck is divine intentionality."[5] Closer examination of the story clearly reveals that Naomi and Ruth engineered almost all the events that later

---

3. Cf. Bellis, *Helpmates Harlots Heroes*, 207.
4. LaCocque, *The Feminine Unconventional*, 100.
5. Trible, *God and the Rhetoric of Sexuality*, 176.

transpired. As Trible comments further, "Under the blessing of God these two women work out their own salvation."[6]

From the point where Ruth goes out to glean in the fields of Boaz, the plot thickens. Neither Boaz nor any other male is in control of events. As Trible notes, "The story belongs to Ruth and Naomi—and to chance, that code for the divine."[7] Or, as Spencer puts it, "While Ruth's world remains thoroughly patriarchal—the whole point is her redemption through marrying a kinsman and bearing his son—Ruth and Naomi, women closely knit in their struggle for survival, take the initiative in creating and nurturing the new familial unit (Boaz is just along for the ride)."[8] Naomi takes charge and instructs Ruth to wait until Boaz has eaten and drunk and "his heart is merry with wine" (Ruth 3:7) and then take note of where he lies down to sleep. After Boaz is asleep Ruth is instructed by Naomi to uncover his "feet" and lie down with him. I have noted previously the use of "feet" as a euphemism for genitals (see above). While this may be shocking to our modern sensibilities, the likelihood is that Ruth uncovered the lower half of Boaz's body.[9]

This was a bold and daring plan, which could easily have resulted in Ruth's being deemed an adulteress, among other things. Imagine Boaz's surprise when he awoke in the middle of the night and found a woman lying beside him who was not there when he went to sleep! And, if all this were not audacious enough, Ruth proposed marriage to Boaz. (At least her words "Spread your covering over your maid, as you are a close relative" [Ruth 3:9b] *may* be understood in this fashion.) In the words of Frederic Bush, "Ruth very understandably did *not* leave the meaning of that moment to Boaz's interpretation of mute metaphors and the inarticulate implications of symbolic action! Rather, she put the meaning of the moment into words and told Boaz what to do."[10] As noted by Trible, this is an interesting reversal, in that in her instructions Naomi had said Boaz would tell *her* what to do.[11] Ruth is clearly the protagonist in the situation. Had she played the role of submissiveness, which was the norm

---

6. Trible, *Texts of Terror*, 85.
7. Trible, *God and the Rhetoric of Sexuality*, 178.
8. F. Scott Spencer, *Dancing Girls*, 83.
9. Ibid, p. 183. Cf. also LaCocque, *The Feminine Unconventional*, 103.
10. Hubbard & Barker, gen. eds., *Ruth, Esther*, 181. Cf. also ibid., 161.
11. Trible, *God and the Rhetoric of Sexuality*, 182.

of her society, the marriage to Boaz in all probability would never have taken place; and the consequences for Israel's history would have been considerable. Boaz and Ruth were the great-grandparents of none other than the great king David. LaCocque refers to Ruth as a savior in a "foreign land," which "happens to be none else than Israel." He further comments, "A work of salvation done on behalf of Israel by a Moabitess is as scandalous as a work of salvation performed by an Israelite prophet on behalf of Nineveh!" (In case anyone should miss the allusion, the reference is to the "prophet" Jonah who, however reluctantly, went to Nineveh and preached a message of God's judgment that resulted in repentance by the Ninevites and the averting of their destruction.) Further, as an indication of the high esteem in which she was held by later generations, Ruth received the additional honor as one of only four women who are mentioned in the genealogy of Jesus as recorded in the Gospel of Matthew (Matt 1:5).

To go into an extended discussion of critical methods of interpreting Ruth and the different readings that this would yield is beyond the scope of this work. I do think it is appropriate, however, to indicate something of the diverse readings of this text by recent scholars. At one end of the spectrum is a reading that sees the book as simply supporting the traditional patriarchy of the age. In the words of Esther Fuchs, "Ruth is held up as a figure of admiration not so much because she returns to the land of Judah with her mother-in-law, or because of her enterprising and intrepid nature, 'but for her success in finding and marrying a direct relative of Elimelech, her father-in-law, and giving birth to children who would carry on the patrilineage of her deceased husband.'"[12] In the light of this claim, I call attention to the fact that Naomi's husband plays no role in the story after the statement of his death in Ruth 1:3 except for the bare mention of his name in Ruth 4:9. When a son is born to Boaz and Ruth, the neighbor women do not say, "A son has been born to Mahlon or Elimelech" (or Boaz), but "A son has been born to Naomi" (Ruth 4:17)! "In that situation shines the silver lining of the cloud of female oppression, of the forced marriage, the utter dependence upon men."[13] As Trible notes, "Nowhere . . . does either woman mention or imply the restoration of a male name. Their emphasis is life for the living."[14] This totally subverts the

---

12. Cited in Murphy, *The Word according to Eve*, 114.
13. Lofts, *Women in the Old Testament*, 95–96.
14. Trible, *God and the Rhetoric of Sexuality*, 193.

rule of levirate marriage.[15] In this story it is the *woman* whose name is passed on, rather than that of the deceased husband.[16]

At the other end of the spectrum from Fuchs are those who see the book of Ruth as a thoroughly subversive document. As Bellis comments "the ruling elite situated in Jerusalem, who wanted to exclude from the Israelite community all foreigners, are being subtly mocked. Ruth's role brings Naomi back to life."[17] Bellis then cites the words of Ilan Pardes,

> There is heroism here, however, of another kind. Without Ruth, Naomi would be a widow without support, without property (at least for all practical purposes), without goal in life ("call me Marah, Bitter," [sic] she says on her way back to Bethlehem.) The Jewess without the Moabitess is but deadwood. Written in the time of Ezra and Nehemiah, the story is a politically subversive pamphlet. No one with the desire to shock his or her Israelite readership could have chosen a "hero" more controversial, even repulsive, than a woman from Moab. Moreover, as if it were not scandalous enough to have that personage of the drama helping and, literally, nourishing an Israelite, the story intends to show that the sociopolitical tension introduced by the unwelcome presence of the foreigner in the community will be resolved, not by the expulsion but by the marriage of the Moabitess with Boaz.[18]

In order to properly appreciate the significance of Pardes's reference to Ruth as being written in the time of Ezra and Nehemiah, let me cite a couple of brief references from the Biblical books by those names. "Then Ezra the priest stood up and said to them, 'You have been unfaithful and have married foreign wives adding to the guilt of Israel. Now, therefore, make confession to the Lord God of your fathers, and do His will; and separate yourselves from the peoples of the land and from the foreign wives'" (Ezra 10:10–11). In another passage Nehemiah says, "In those days I also saw that the Jews had married women from Ashdod, Ammon *and* Moab. As for their children, half spoke in the language of Ashdod, and none of them was able to speak the language of Judah, but the language

---

15. This is the law providing that, if a man died childless, his brother or next of kin was supposed to marry the widow, and the first son born was to be given the name of the deceased, so as to carry on his name.

16. Cf. Trible, *Texts of Terror*, 85; LaCocque, *The Feminine Unconventional*, 94–95: Parales, *Hidden Voices*, 28.

17. Bellis, *Helpmates Harlots Heroes*, 208.

18. Ibid.

of his own people. So I contended with them and cursed them and struck some of them and pulled out their hair, and made them swear by God, 'You shall not give your daughters to their sons, nor take of their daughters for your sons or for yourselves'" (Neh 13:23–25).

From a consideration of these passages alone, the scandalous nature of the story of Ruth can be seen, if in fact it was written during the time of Ezra and Nehemiah. Not only is Ruth the heroine of this story, but she is placed in the lineage of the one who is presented in the Jewish Scriptures as the most idealized of all the kings of Israel, none other than David![19]

Recent interpreters have developed an almost endless variety of interpretations of the book of Ruth. I have chosen only to present the two extremes in the range of recent interpretations. As with most sets of extremes, the truth is probably found somewhere in between.

---

19. Although a later tradition, *Ruth Rabbah*, presents David as complaining that his foes consider his descent from Ruth the Moabitess as "tainted." (Cited in LaCocque, *The Feminine Unconventional*, 107 n. 58.)

17

Naomi

OBVIOUSLY THE STORY OF Naomi is so intertwined with that of Ruth that it has already been covered to a large degree. I believe, however, that she deserves treatment on her own merits.

First of all, she clearly represents a departure from the narrow-minded nationalism that the Jewish Scriptures depict repeatedly. We see no sign whatever of any prejudice toward either Ruth or Orpah because of their being Moabites, even though in most periods of history the Moabites had been enemies of Israel. She reflects a strong concern for their welfare after the death of her sons, even if she is somewhat limited in her understanding of what was in their best interests. As noted earlier, she sees their welfare in terms of finding a husband among their own people (Ruth 1:9). It remains for Ruth to open Naomi's eyes to other possibilities.

A measure of the character of Naomi is that, while she knew she was related to Boaz, and that he was a person of considerable wealth (Ruth 2:1), she never went to him for a handout. (Nor, as Trible has noted, had Boaz visited her, although he was aware of her plight.[1]) Instead, Naomi chose to accept Ruth's offer to go and glean in the grain fields that were being harvested. Israelite tradition mandated that the corners of the fields, and the grain that was accidentally dropped during the harvesting, should be left for the needy and the *ger* ("stranger") (Lev 19:9–10). Ruth qualified to glean on both counts: she was needy and a stranger in an unknown land.

Naomi is presented as a woman of insight and decisive action, qualities much more associated with males in her society than with females. Caspi and Cohen highlight this quality in the following words: "She has received the call, has taken it upon herself to save her family name, has

---

1. Trible, *God and the Rhetoric of Sexuality*, 179.

Naomi

removed herself from a place of evil and arriving (*sic*) in Bethlehem, we at last have a hint of what is within her."[2] Approaching the story rhetorically, Trible notes that in Ruth 2 the story begins with Ruth speaking to Naomi and ends with Naomi speaking to Ruth. The speaking of Ruth and Naomi encircle the story of Ruth's gleaning in the field. "Moreover, design and content yield a feminist interpretation: in their own right the women shape their story. They plan (v. 2); they execute (vv. 3–17); and they evaluate (vv. 18–22). But this symmetry is also asymmetrical. Whereas the young woman takes command at first, the old woman outstrips—not matches—her at last. Much longer than the dialogic introduction, the conclusion moves back and forth between these two females until it stops, where it started, with Naomi."[3]

Naomi's plan for Ruth to uncover the "feet" of Boaz and to lie down with him after he had gone to sleep has been noted above. Her plan was bold and masterful, which succeeded in exceptional fashion. Although I would make no attempt to deny that Naomi is in one sense the victim of traditional patriarchy, and hence has to resort to some trickery instead of dealing with her problem in a direct manner, she nevertheless devised and carried out a plan that thoroughly subverted that patriarchy.[4]

---

2. Caspi & Cohen, *Still Waters Run Deep*, 101.
3. Trible, *God and the Rhetoric of Sexuality*, 180–81.
4. Cf. Berquist, *Reclaiming Her Story*, 152–53.

18

Abigail

THE STORY OF ABIGAIL and David somewhat bears out Stanton's comment that "The chief business of the women in the reigns of Kings Saul and David seems to have been to rescue men from the craft and the greed of each other."[1] It is set during the time that David is fleeing from Saul, who is still determined to kill him in order to get rid of a rival claimant to the throne of Israel. David has by this time attracted several hundred ne'er-do-wells as followers (1 Sam 22:20). He and his men were hiding out in the Judean highlands in a place just west of the Dead Sea and south of Jerusalem. A wealthy shepherd named Nabal was in the area who had a wife named Abigail (1 Sam 25:2–3). David had protected Nabal's property all the time he and his men were present so that Nabal lost nothing (1 Sam 25:7). When time came for Nabal to shear his sheep, David sent messengers to Nabal, suggesting that the "police protection" he had provided to Nabal deserved a reward. Nabal answered this request in a churlish and insulting manner. He insinuated that David was nothing more than a rebel who had broken away from his rightful master and did not deserve anything from him (1 Sam 25:9–10). In response, David instructed his four hundred followers to put on their swords and follow him to the place where Nabal was encamped.

In the meantime, one of the male servants informed Abigail as to what Nabal had done. He reminded her that David and his followers had been very good to them, and that they had lost no property since David came on the scene (1 Sam 25:14–16). At this point we get an interesting insight into Nabal's character. The young man says evil is coming their way, and Nabal is such a *ben-beli'al* (literally, "son of worthlessness"—

---

1. Stanton, *The Woman's Bible*, II:51.

Abigail

a rough modern equivalent would be "son of a bitch") that no one can speak to him (1 Sam 25:17)!

Upon receiving this information Abigail sprang into action. She began to load large quantities of food upon donkeys (1 Sam 25:18). After sending her young men on ahead of her with the "bribe," she mounted a donkey and rode out to meet David (1 Sam 25:20). When she came face to face with him, she dismounted from her donkey and addressed him in the most submissive of terms. As Bellis has noted, "She constantly speaks of herself in very lowly terms, calling herself maidservant (*'amha*) and handmaid (*sipha*). These terms stand in contrast to the power she wields through her words. She effectively prevents David from attacking her husband and his men and she links herself with David."[2] To paraphrase part of her words, she said, "Don't pay any attention to my husband Nabal. His name means 'fool'—and he lives up to it" (1 Sam 25:23-25)! David responded to her by saying that the God of Israel should be praised for sending her out to meet him that day and keeping him from bloodshed (1 Sam 25:32-33).

When Abigail returned to her tent, she found Nabal in the midst of a party and too drunk to understand anything she might tell him (1 Sam 25:36). When she told Nabal the next morning about his narrow escape from being killed by David, he seems to have had a heart attack and gone into a coma. Ten days later he died. (I am basing this on 1 Sam 25:37-38. I will let the reader judge as to the accuracy of this interpretation.) When David heard that Nabal was dead, he sent some of his servants to Abigail to request that she become his wife. As Bilezekian puts it, "When David learned that Nabal was dead, he praised the Lord and married the beautiful widow."[3] (How many wives David already had at this point is difficult to determine. He seems to have taken Ahinoam of Jezreel as a wife about this same time, and we know that Michal had at one time been his wife [1 Sam 25:43-44]. Second Samuel 3:1-4 lists six wives, and we know that Bathsheba became his wife some time after he became king of Israel.)

Abigail's quick thinking and resolute action clearly prevented David from killing her husband and all his male servants (cf. 1 Sam 25:21-22).[4] She had neither a sword nor any army behind her. Surely a story of great-

---

2. Bellis, *Helpmates Harlots Heroes* 148; Cf. Bach, ed., *The Pleasure of Her Text*, 25-34.
3. Bilezikian, *Beyond Sex Roles*, 73.
4. Cf. Berquist, *Reclaiming Her Story*, 112.

er courage than she exhibited would be very difficult to find. Although Abigail was a woman trapped in a very patriarchal society she refused to acknowledge the limitations that society attempted to place on her. As Gretchen Hull has noted, "She had the inner strength to perceive that David had embarked on a disastrous course of action and to rebuke him for it. Her tactful but forceful words of wisdom prevented him from a rash act." A little further on, after mentioning Miriam, Rahab, Jael, Deborah, Huldah, and the wise woman of Proverbs 31, Hull commented: "Like Abigail, these women were not locked into some sort of artificial role playing nor were they limited by the men in their lives. They lived in a patriarchal society, but they operated in non-patriarchal ways, and the Bible text [sic] commends them for their actions."[5] In the words of Parales, "She defied her husband's poor decision, acted independently, and sent supplies out to David. Hardly a submissive wife, Abigail saved her own life and that of her whole household—except for her husband. God blessed her for her wisdom and diplomatic skill."[6] Katherine Bushnell, perhaps the earliest of all feminist scholars, wrote, "The whole Bible story goes to show that Abigail did the right and prudent thing in going against what she well knew was her husband's will, to do what she could not have done with his knowledge. She showed moral courage. She averted a dire calamity. David praised her for it."[7]

Some words from Nunnally-Cox are worth quoting at some length:

> She (Abigail) breaks social codes, and does mostly as she pleases. One would suspect that she was the true household manager, for no one objects when she packs up a large quantity of food and rides to meet a young stranger. Having lived with an irascible man for several years, she is not about to have her household razed under her for Nabal's lack of sense. Abigail herself seems to have a good, quick sense, and when opportunity comes to escape the ordinary, she loses no time in saddling her ass to become David's wife. She leaves behind both the proper period for mourning and a very wealthy household. Here is a woman who enjoys ordering her own life.[8]

---

5. Hull, *Equal to Serve*, 111, 113. See also Brenner, *The Israelite Woman*, 39–42.
6. Parales, *Hidden Voices*, 25.
7. Bushnell, *God's Word to Women*, 20:150.
8. Nunnally-Cox, *Foremothers*, 73.

19

Michal

THE STORY OF MICHAL takes us into the beginning stages of the Israelite kingdom. Michal is the younger daughter of Saul, the first king of Israel. Saul had first promised, then withheld, his older daughter Merab from David (1 Sam 18:17–19). We then read that Michal loved David, and Saul thought he saw a way to rid himself of a competitor who was already being recognized as the one who would take over the kingdom after him (1 Sam 18:20–21). When David protested that he was poor and unworthy to become the king's son-in-law, Saul suggested that in place of the traditional bride price David bring him the foreskins of one hundred Philistines. Saul's apparent hope was that David would be killed by the Philistines when he tried to collect this "bride price" (1 Sam 18:25). Saul was to be disappointed, however, because David collected not one hundred but two hundred Philistine foreskins. (Josephus says the "bride price" was to be six hundred *heads* of Philistines, and that David readily produced them.[1] One wonders if perhaps there is really no contradiction here, other than the numbers [and Josephus is so well known for inflating numbers as not to require further comment], but that Josephus was thinking of heads of penises instead of literal heads in the usual sense.) Obviously, Saul had no choice but to give Michal to David as a wife (1 Sam 18:27).

From this point, the story is one of Saul's increasing suspicion and fear of David, and of Saul's trying in a variety of ways to put David to death. The Biblical writer says that an evil spirit from God came upon Saul (1 Sam 18:10).[2] "And if one chooses to understand that, as middle

---

1. *Antiquities* vi.x.ii–iii.

2. Looking at the story as a whole, I would suggest that Saul had become a manic-depressive, but of course no means of diagnosing such an illness was available to the ancient writer. Everything that happened was attributed directly to God. No allowance

age encroached, Saul lost his vigour [sic] and his ambition and his courage and drifted into a form of melancholia not far removed from madness, that is only putting the same situation into another mould of words."[3]

After twice failing to kill David with a spear, Saul finally had David's house surrounded at night and commanded that David be put to death the next morning (1 Sam 19:11a). This is where Michal again comes into the picture. She was well aware of what her father was trying to do, and she let David down by a rope through the window of their house and advised him to flee for his life (1 Sam 19:11b–12). This raises an obvious question as to how she could accomplish this without Saul's men seeing her and rushing in to capture David before he could get away. One possibility is that David's house, like that of Rahab (see above) was in the city wall and that his being lowered from the window placed him outside the city.[4]

Michal's next act is to take one of the household gods, place it in David's bed, and (apparently) wrap a quilt of goats' hair around its head and cover it with bedclothes.[5] The next morning, when Saul's men came to take David, Michal told them that he was sick and unable to come to Saul (1 Sam 19:13–14). When Saul heard this, he ordered David to be brought to him, on his bed if necessary, so that he could put him to death (1 Sam 19:15). Only then is the deception discovered. Saul promptly challenged Michal as to how she could deceive her father and let his enemy escape.

---

was made for what we would call secondary causation or human freedom of choice at this early period in the history of Israel.

3. Lofts, *Women in the Old Testament*, 98.
4. See, e.g., Hubbard and Barker, eds., *1 Samuel*, 197.
5. The Hebrew text is very difficult to translate at this point. It reflects Michal's placing something pertaining to a goat at the teraphim's head, but no one knows for sure exactly what that "something" was. The translators of the Septuagint, the Greek version of the Jewish Scriptures, have Michal placing a goat's liver in David's bed. The Jewish historian Josephus has followed the Septuagint, prompting William Whiston, the translator of Josephus' writings, to argue strongly for the correctness of this translation. (See *Antiquities* vi.xi.iv and notes thereunto.) Whiston's argument is that the translation "goat's liver" is quite logical, in that it's being placed in the location where David's head was assumed to be would have caused the covers to move in a way which simulated the irregular breathing of a sick man. I don't profess to be an expert on goat's livers, but my guess is that only a very fresh one would have any movement to it. If this be true, one's imagination is almost stretched to the breaking point in trying to explain how, with Saul's men watching the house on all sides, Michal (or anyone else) could have gone out and slain a goat and brought the liver into the house without arousing suspicions. Maybe I am just a die-hard traditionalist, but I still think a pillow or quilt made of goat's hair makes more sense here!

This forced her to fabricate another lie and say that David had threatened to kill her if she did not help him escape (1 Sam 19:17).

I will leave aside any question as to the ethics of Michal's deception and focus on the courage and ingenuity she exhibited. In Exum's words, "*In the story told to us* Michal is the agent, the active character who executes the plan: she warns David, she lets him down through the window, she puts the teraphim in David's bed and tells her father's messengers that David is sick, and she responds to Saul's accusation that *she let David escape*" (emphasis original).[6] She placed her life on the line to save the life of the man she loved. (Whether or not David loved Michal is an open question—the text never explicitly says that David returned her love.[7]) As Laffey aptly points out, "As David's wife, she used prudence, courage, and cunning to save him from her father's pursuit and from almost-certain [*sic*] death. Interpreters are accustomed to laud the character of men who act with such bravery; readers must begin to laud the character of such women also."[8]

From this point, Michal's life takes some rather tortuous turns, and the worst features of her society's patriarchy come to the fore. After David's escape, her father gave her as a wife to one Palti (1 Sam 25:44). Years of intrigue followed in which David was a fugitive from Saul. Then, after Saul's death, his army commander Abner offered to turn the kingdom over to David. David agreed, on the condition that Michal be brought back to him (2 Sam 3:12–13). Again, whether David loved Michal, or whether he wanted the political benefits of joining the "house of Saul" to the "house of David" may be debated. At any rate, Saul's son Ish-bosheth takes Michal away from Palti(el) forcibly and brings her to David. Michal is thus reduced to mere property to be dispensed in any manner the males in power desired.

The final appearance of Michal occurs when David is consolidating his kingdom and is in the process of establishing Jerusalem as his capital city. After an abortive attempt to use the Ark of the Covenant to guarantee victory over the Philistines, it had been left at Kiriath-Jearim (see 1 Sam 4:3—7:2). David decided to transport the Ark to Jerusalem by ox cart. On the trip, the cart almost overturned and a man named

---

6. Exum, *Fragmented Women*, 49.

7. For an argument that David's motive for wanting Michal as his wife was strictly political, see Berquist, *Remembering Her Story*, 107–9.

8. Cited in Bellis, *Helpmates Harlots Heroes*, 146.

Uzzah put out his hand to steady the Ark and was struck dead (2 Sam 6:6–7). For three months the Ark remained at the house of a man named Obed-edom. When word reached David that the presence of the Ark had brought blessings to the house of Obed-edom, he decided to try a second time to bring it to Jerusalem (2 Sam 6:10–12). This time he was successful, and David led the procession into the city of Jerusalem, dancing as he went; and apparently with very little clothing on his body (2 Sam 6:14)! Michal looked out her window and saw this procession, which she clearly thought was lacking in dignity. She chided David for exposing himself in this manner with women looking on (2 Sam 6:20). The account closes with the somber statement that Michal died childless (2 Sam 6:24).

How are we to understand this statement that Michal died childless? "Closing of the womb" so that a woman could not bear children was usually presented as an act of Yahweh, and often as Yahweh's *punishment* for some action or other (cf. Gen 16:2, 20:18, 30:2; 1 Sam 1:5). This may be what the present text has in view. Alternatively, it may simply mean that David never again had sexual relations with Micah. Exum has noted that, read on one level, Michal's fabricated story that David threatened to kill her may have contained a grain of truth. "Michal's literary murder in 2 Samuel 6 at the hand of the androcentric narrator—by means of David's words and the hint that David may be responsible for Michal's childlessness—would make it seem that David's threat to kill Michal has now been carried out."[9] In other words, it was psychological death for a woman in that society not to bear children (cf. Luke 1:24–25).

In entertaining such questions we must not lose sight of the courage demonstrated by Michal in this series of events. She confronted the man who was both her husband and the king of all Israel. Either role would have given him complete authority over her. Her rebuke of David could have resulted in her death—either psychologically or literally. As Exum aptly notes,

> Michal's going out to confront David is an act of self-assertion. Such boldness on her part cannot be tolerated; the narrator lets her protest but robs her of voice at the critical moment, allowing her no reply to David and no further speech. Whereas the narrator uses Michal's protest to eliminate her, her protest can be used against the narrator to bring to light the crime, to expose the gender bias of the story. By speaking out, Michal lays claim to her own

---

9. Exum, *Fragmented Women*, 50.

story. She cannot avoid her fate, but she can protest it. She goes to her literary death screaming, as it were. Her protest thus serves as an indictment of the phallogocentric world view represented in and reflected by the narrative.[10]

---

10. Bach, ed., "Murder They Wrote," 61.

20

Bathsheba

The story of Bathsheba is given in several short scenes in 2 Samuel 11–12 and 1 Kings 1–2. She first appears as a beautiful woman who lived close enough to King David's palace that he was able to see her bathing from his roof (2 Sam 11: 2). David liked what he saw and inquired as to who the woman was. He was told that she was Bathsheba, the wife of Uriah the Hittite (2 Sam 11:3). David then had Bathsheba brought to the palace and had sexual relations with her (2 Sam 11:4).

Bathsheba is totally silenced throughout this succession of events. We get no insight whatever concerning her feelings or desires. She is simply one man's property being taken over by another, more powerful, man. She offered no resistance, probably recognizing that any resistance would be futile. Traditional patriarchy has often laid the blame on Bathsheba for her adultery, as if she had deliberately placed herself in view of David in order to get his attention. In the words of Winter, "The traditional interpretation of Bathsheba's story presents her as a woman who got into trouble through her own beauty, her own fault. Bathsheba might tell a different story, one that presents her as a victim of a powerful king."[1] Bellis, in a similar vein, comments, "Although Bathsheba is often condemned as a seductress, there is nothing in the text that suggests her complicity in David's crime. Quite the contrary. She appears to be an innocent victim of his lust. . . . How she feels about the rape, for that is what it may have been, we are not told."[2] Any active role that Bathsheba may have had has to be conjectured. There is absolutely nothing in the Biblical text to support this. Her victimization by a powerful king *is* supported in the text. As Gretchen Hull has commented, "He (David) simply lusted after a pretty

---

1. Winter, *Bathsheba*.
2. Bellis, *Helpmates Harlots Heroes*, 149.

woman, forcibly seized her, and when she became pregnant, cold-bloodedly arranged for the murder of her husband. When male supremacy ruled, might made right and people were throwaways. God disciplined David, but not Bathsheba, although of course she, too, suffered when their first child died."[3]

Bathsheba's silence is finally broken when she sends word to David that she is pregnant. Her husband Uriah is with David's army as they make war against Rabbah, a city of the Ammonites (1 Sam 11:1, cf. 12:26). In an attempt to cover up his sin, David had Uriah brought back to Jerusalem and suggested that he go to his house and "wash his feet" (2 Sam 11:6–8). I have previously noted the usage of the word "feet" as a euphemism for the sexual organs (see above). David was clearly hoping that Uriah would have sexual relations with his wife so that the child would appear to be his, but he did not reckon with Uriah's integrity. When David got word the next day that Uriah had not gone to his house, but had slept at the door of the palace all night, he asked Uriah for an explanation. Uriah answered, to paraphrase, "What right do I have to enjoy the comforts of my house and my wife when all my fellow soldiers are camped in the field under battle conditions (2 Sam 11:9–11)?" Thus far David's carefully conceived (pun intended!) plan is not working, so he has to try again. He asks Uriah to stay around another night before returning to the battlefield. David then "wined and dined" Uriah in the hope that excessive drinking would make him unable to resist the temptation to go home to his wife (2 Sam 11:12–14). Still Uriah refused to go to his house, and David began to get more and more desperate. Finally, he gave Uriah a note to be delivered to Joab, the captain of David's army, which instructed Joab to place Uriah in the most dangerous place possible and then withdraw from him and so make sure that he would be killed (2 Sam 11:14–15). Uriah unwittingly carried the notice of his own death sentence to the man who would carry it out. The unscrupulous Joab seems not to have even questioned this order and promptly complied with it (2 Sam 11:16–17). As soon as the period of mourning for Uriah was over, David had Bathsheba brought to the palace to become his wife (2 Sam 11:27). Once again Bathsheba's voice is silenced and we have no way of knowing whether she became David's wife willingly or because she had no choice.

---

3. Hull, *Equal to Serve*, 94.

In this manner David completed the cover-up of his sin, or so he thought. The Biblical writer, however, tells us that God was not pleased with David's actions. God immediately sent Nathan the prophet to rebuke David with the story about a rich man with great flocks and herds who took a poor man's only ewe lamb to serve to his guests (2 Sam 11:27—12:4). When David's anger mounted against the rich man in Nathan's story, Nathan said, "You are the man" (2 Sam 12:7). As a consequence of his adultery with Bathsheba, David was told that the child would surely die (2 Sam 12:14).

The next glimpse we get of Bathsheba comes shortly after the death of the child begotten by David. David is said to have comforted Bathsheba and had sexual relations with her so that another child was born. David named him "peaceful one" (Solomon) (2 Sam 12:24).

We hear no more of Bathsheba until shortly before the time of David's death. In the previous glimpses we had into Bathsheba's life, she was in the traditional role of the submissive woman who accepted fully the authority of the men in her life. The final glimpses of her in the Bible, however, show her in a considerably different light. Though we may have to do a bit of reading between the lines to see it, she emerges as a woman of authority who plays a major role in the selection of the one who will inherit David's throne.

A power struggle had developed just before David's death and it lasted for several years before it was completely settled. David's son Adonijah proclaimed himself king and invited a large number of prominent citizens to celebrate his becoming king (1 Kgs 1:5-9). The biblical author says Adonijah "exalted himself" to be king (1 Kgs 1:5). Actually, he seems to have had a legitimate claim to be David's successor. He was born after Absalom, whom Joab had killed (1 Kgs 1:6, cf. 2 Sam 18:1-15). With Absalom out of the way, he was now David's oldest son. David, however, for reasons we are not told, had promised that Solomon would be his successor. (Or, as Exum has suggested, Nathan and Bathsheba may have duped David into believing that he had made such a promise, as there is no hint of such a promise in the text.[4])

Nathan the prophet then came to Bathsheba and persuaded her to go in to David and "remind" him of his promise that Solomon would be king, and ask why Adonijah was now proclaiming himself king (1 Kgs 1:11-13).

---

4. Exum, *Fragmented Women*, 198-99.

As soon as she had had time to speak to David, Nathan promised to come in and verify her words (1 Kgs 1:14). Here we begin to suspect that there is more to the story than meets the eye. Why involve Bathsheba? Nathan had not hesitated to confront David directly in the matter of his adultery. Why would he not confront David directly concerning this matter? Could it be that he knew Bathsheba had now become the "power behind the throne?" In the words of Caspi and Cohen, "The help she received from Nathan the Prophet [sic] accentuates the power she accumulated during the years as a queen and attracts the attention of the reader, allowing Bathsheba to be seen in a different light. Here, in her involvement to make her son the heir and the support she gets from the people close to the king announces to the reader that from the beginning, Bathsheba was crowned with success and with it accumulates power to control the king's court and the old king's decisions."[5]

However we may interpret the text, David listened to Bathsheba and Nathan and affirmed that Solomon would replace him as king (1 Kgs 1:29–30). He immediately summoned Zadok the priest, Nathan the prophet, and Benaiah to him (1 Kgs 1:32). He instructed them to place Solomon on his personal mule, go down to the Gihon Spring, and there anoint Solomon as king (1 Kgs 1:33–34).

Bathsheba then drops out of the picture for awhile, to reappear as Solomon is attempting to establish his kingship. Though Adonijah had temporarily given up on any attempt to become king, he clearly did not give up permanently. He came to Bathsheba one day and asked her to request something from Solomon. Once again, this would seem to indicate that Bathsheba exerted considerable influence on the Israelite throne. Adonijah's request was that he be given Abishag the Shunammite as a wife (1 Kgs 2:13–17). Abishag was a young virgin who had been brought to David in his old age to (euphemistically) "keep him warm" (1 Kgs 1:1–4). Despite the statement that David did not cohabit with her, she would have become his property. If Adonijah took Abishag as his wife, this would have said to the people that he was taking over David's throne. Whether Bathsheba was naïve and simply did not recognize his designs, or whether she allowed herself to be manipulated, is impossible to say. Some have argued that she knew perfectly well the implications of Adonijah's request and saw this as a means of getting rid of a major rival of her son

---

5. Caspi and Cohen, *Still Waters Run Deep*, 53–54.

permanently—and perhaps getting some revenge upon Abishag, who had come between her and David, as well.[6] (Abishag drops out of the narrative at this point, and we are never told what her fate was.[7]) Adele Berlin has voiced such an explanation in these words: "Bathsheba is really hateful. She wants to get Adonijah out of the way. She knows that Solomon will react negatively to the request. Thus she sets up the situation in which he will be killed."[8] Whatever may have been her motives, Bathsheba conveyed the request to her son Solomon, who clearly was *not* naïve about the matter (1 Kgs 2:22)! He promptly sent Benaiah to execute Adonijah (1 Kgs 2:25).

Despite Bathsheba's passive role in so much of the story, we should not lose track of the fact that Nathan the prophet and Adonijah both clearly believed that she could influence kings David and Solomon. Further, when Bathsheba came to Solomon to relay Adonijah's request, he rose up to meet her, *bowed down to her*, then sat on his throne and *had a throne for her* placed on his right. He then promised to give her whatever she requested (1 Kgs 2:19–20). Some English versions read "He had a *seat* (or chair) placed for his mother," instead of a throne. The same Hebrew word is used for Solomon's throne and for the place where his mother sat, however, so it is rather arbitrary to translate the same word two different ways in the same sentence. Furthermore, in the ancient world the right hand was symbolic of power, so Bathsheba is symbolically placed in the position of executing the power of Solomon.[9] Bathsheba is no longer the property of a man who can do with her as he pleases. To be sure, Solomon went back on his word and did not grant her request. He could not have granted that request, however, without giving up the kingdom (which Bathsheba herself had helped him to gain). Thus we can see that Bathsheba has evolved from a submissive, voiceless victim of male patriarchy into a woman whose influence extends to the seat of power in Israel. How much of her story has remained forever untold we can only guess. We are told just enough to see that there must have been much more to the story. From the little we *are* told of her story, she eventually emerges as a strong woman of power and influence. Her characterization by Lofts

---

6. See, for example, ibid., 61–62.
7. Ibid.
8. Cited in Bellis, *Helpmates Harlots Heroes*, 161.
9. Cf. Hubbard & Barker, eds., *1 Kings*, 38.

Bathsheba

as a puppet who never did anything except what some man ordered her to do is far wide of the mark, in my judgment.[10]

---

10. Lofts, *Women in the Old Testament*, 121.

21

Jezebel

PERHAPS NO FEMALE NAME in history carries as many negative connotations as does Jezebel. Her story is embedded at various points in 1 Kings 16–21 and 2 Kings 9. These books are a part of a larger section known as the Deuteronomic History (or Deuteronomistic History, as some scholars prefer to call it) that extends from Deuteronomy–2 Kings.[1]

Jezebel is first introduced as wife of King Ahab of Israel and the daughter of Ethbaal, king of Sidon (1 Kgs 16:31). The historian seems to indicate that Ahab's marriage to Jezebel was on a par with "walking in the sins of Jeroboam, son of Nebat." She appears to have tried to completely wipe out the prophets of Yahweh, and she succeeded except for one hundred who were hidden by a man named Obadiah (not the same prophet as in the Biblical book by that name) [1 Kgs 18:4, 13]. We later learn that Jezebel imported 850 pagan "prophets" from her native country and fed them at the royal table (1 Kgs 18:19). The story of Elijah's challenge to these prophets is well known. When the prophets' god was unable to answer by fire, Elijah had them all rounded up and slaughtered (1 Kgs 18:21–40).

The next development is that Jezebel vowed to treat Elijah like he had treated her prophets (1 Kgs 19:2). Elijah, in fear, headed for the wil-

---

1. This history is thought to have begun in the reign of Josiah, c. 641–609 BCE. It reflects a distinct bias against the Northern Kingdom, Israel, which separated from Judah following the death of Solomon. Israel never had a descendant of David on its throne and so, in the mind of the southern historian, it was never a legitimate kingdom. The first king, Jereboam son of Nebat, was the "yardstick" by which all the kings of Israel were measured by the "D" historian. (See, for example 1 Kings 16:26, 31; 2 Kings 2:2–3, 13:2, 6,11; 14:24, 15:9, 18, 24, 28: 17:21; cf. also Brenner, *The Israelite Woman*, 22. [Page citations are to the reprint edition.]) We should thus be on the alert, not only for gender bias, but also bias against the rulers of Israel.

derness of Beersheba in Judah (1 Kgs 19:3). (Enough sarcastic remarks have been made concerning the fact that Elijah was totally unafraid before eight hundred fifty male prophets but ran from one woman that I will add nothing to the list!)

Jezebel reappears in the story in the infamous episode concerning Naboth's vineyard (1 Kgs 21:1–16). Ahab attempted to buy or trade for Naboth's vineyard, but the latter refused, saying it was the inheritance of his fathers. Ahab went home and pouted! When Jezebel found him in such a mood she inquired as to the reason. When Ahab explained, she immediately took matters into her own hands. She wrote letters in Ahab's name and sealed them with his seal. Those letters instructed that Naboth was to be brought up on charges of cursing God. False witnesses were to testify against him, and then he was to be taken out and stoned to death. She then told Ahab that Naboth was dead, and that he could now take possession of the vineyard. When he does so, he encounters the prophet Elijah, who informs him that the dogs will eat Jezebel in the same location where Naboth was killed (1 Kgs 21:23).

We hear no more of Jezebel until the point when Jehu begins to take over the Northern Kingdom, Israel. Jehu rides out to Jezreel, which seems to have been Ahab's capital city (1 Kgs 18:45–46). Jezebel learned that he was coming, and "she painted her eyes and adorned her head" in preparation (2 Kgs 9:30). This somewhat strange detail gives rise to a number of questions. Did Jezebel think that if she appeared beautiful, Jehu might spare her life? Did she entertain some hope that he might allow her to remain as queen? Unfortunately for us, these questions did not concern the Biblical historian. We can only conjecture what may have motivated Jezebel to act as she did.

Her next act is even more difficult to understand. She leaned out the window and shouted down insultingly, "Is it well, Zimri, your master's murderer" (2 Kgs 9:31)? (Zimri had become king by murdering Elah [1 Kgs 16:8–10]. After reigning for only seven days [1Kgs 16:15], Zimri was replaced by Omri, the father of Ahab; so these events would have been a very recent memory.) "And the words would fall, as she knew they would fall, cold and ominous upon the ear of a man flushed with victory. For Zimri too had been a soldier, a leader of the chariots; Zimri too had slain his king and completely exterminated the royal house. . . . Nothing the woman could have said could have been more pertinent, more mocking, more disturbing."[2]

Jehu responded to Jezebel's taunt by looking up to the window and asking who was on his side. When three "officials" looked down at him he told them to throw Jezebel out the window (2 Kgs 9:32a). Jehu then apparently drove his chariots over her, and went into the house to eat a meal. In the course of the meal he said, in effect, "That old girl was a queen after all—so I guess we can at least give her a burial!" When some of Jehu's men went out to bury her body, the dogs had eaten all but her skull and a few assorted body parts. The Biblical historian then reminds us that Elijah had prophesied these events (2 Kgs 9:32b–37).

Taken at face value, this story is one of grievous sin and divine retribution brought upon a woman who was the epitome of evil. But I again raise the question as to how much of her story has been obscured by gender bias and bias against all the rulers of Israel. Let us look at the story more closely and see if a different picture of Jezebel can be found.

For starters, Jezebel was clearly a literate woman, something unusual for her day.[3] In the affair of Naboth's vineyard she wrote *letters* to some of the local citizenry explaining to them what she wanted done. She appears to have been delegated certain responsibilities for internal affairs by her husband. The text says nothing about her being given Ahab's seal for the above-mentioned letters. It seems she at least had considerable freedom of action in some matters. She was a woman of resolute action, however negatively we may deem her actions.

Jezebel's authority probably stemmed from a twofold base. First, she was the daughter of a Sidonian king and may have been an official priestess of Baal.[4] As such, she would have been educated from birth to govern.[5] Along with this, Jezebel was clearly a woman of economic means, as indicated by the support of the eight hundred fifty prophets of Baal at *her* table (not Ahab's).[6] Second, she had the backing of her husband's authority. Although the Biblical text is silent on this, Ahab may not have wanted to waste her education and talents as the daughter of a king and

---

2. Lofts, *Women in the Old Testament*, 155.
3. For an extended discussion of this issue, see Bar-Ilan, *Some Jewish Women*, 31–51.
4. For a fuller discussion of this, see Brenner, *The Israelite Woman*, 23–27.
5. Ibid., 25.
6. Cf. ibid., 22.

Jezebel

the priestess of a religion. This could explain his delegating certain administrative tasks to her, as indicated by her possession of his seal. How much of Jezebel's own personality may have contributed to her authority we can only imagine. Although her actions are consistently presented in a negative light by the Biblical historian, she was clearly a woman of resolute action. When Jezebel found Ahab pouting because Naboth refused to sell or trade his vineyard, she immediately took charge and told him she would get the vineyard for him. Although in Israel, as Ahab knew full well, Naboth was within his rights in not giving up the inheritance of his fathers. No such rights existed in Jezebel's native land. The monarch took whatever he/she wanted—period. Her action would not have been questioned in her society. As Camp puts it, "Her brutal response to Naboth's refusal to sell his vineyard may be understood from her point of view as an appropriate royal response to insubordination, in contrast to Ahab's unconscionable weakness as a leader."[7]

Much of the Ahab/Jezebel story is presented vis a vis the prophet Elijah. Again, the Biblical historian gives us a "black and white" picture of Elijah as the righteous representative of the true God and Jezebel as the pagan temptress leading Israel away from that God. Jezebel would have seen matters much differently. In her mind she and Elijah were leaders of rival religions. Neither of them showed any mercy to the prophets of the other's religion. Bellis notes that, "Although we may prefer Elijah's God to Jezebel's, Elijah and Jezebel use the same means to accomplish their identical ends. Both are intent on wiping out the other's religion."[8] As Gains puts it, "Ironically, at the conclusion of the Carmel episode, Elijah proves capable of the same murderous inclinations that have previously characterized Jezebel, though it is only she that the Deuteronomist [sic] criticizes."[9] She goes on to suggest that, "Perhaps the biblical compiler is using Jezebel as a scapegoat for his outrage at her influence over the king, meaning that she herself is being framed in the tale."[10] Gaines concludes by saying that "there is much to admire in this ancient queen. In a kinder analysis, Jezebel emerges as a fiery and determined person, with an intensity matched only by Elijah's. She is true to her native religion and

---

7. Cited in Bellis, *Helpmates Harlots Heroes*, 165; Cf. Lofts, *Women in the Old Testament*, 151.

8. Bellis, *Helpmates Harlots Heroes*, 165.

9. Gaines, "How Bad Was Jezebel?," 17.

10. Ibid, 19.

customs. She is even more loyal to her husband. Throughout her reign, she boldly exercises what power she has. And in the end, having lived her life on her own terms, Jezebel faces certain death with dignity."[11]

Ellen Battelle Dietrick has anticipated much of the conclusions of recent feminist scholars. Her somewhat tongue-in-cheek remarks are worth quoting at some length:

> All we know about Jezebel is told us by a rival religionist, who hated her as the Pope of Rome hated Martin Luther, or as an American A. P. A. now hates a Roman Catholic. Nevertheless, even the Jewish historian, evidently biassed [sic] against Jezebel by his theological prejudices as he is, does not give any facts whatever which warrant the assertion that Jezebel was any more satanic than the ancient Israelitish [sic] gentleman, to whom her theological views were opposed. Of course we, at this stage of scientific thought, know that Jezebel's religion was not an admirable one. Strangely enough, for a religion, it actually made her intolerant! But to Jezebel it was a truth, for which she battled as bravely as Elijah did for what he imagined to be eternal verity. The facts, admitted even by the historian who hated her, prove that, notwithstanding her unfortunate and childish conception of theology, Jezebel was a brave, fearless, generous woman, so wholly devoted to her own husband that even wrong seemed justifiable to her, if she could thereby make him happy ... I submit, that if Jezebel is a disgrace to womankind, our dear brethren at any rate have not much cause to be proud of Elijah, so, possibly, we might strike a truce over the character of these two long-buried worthies. It may be well, though, to note here that the now most offensive epithet which the English translators attached to Jezebel's name, originally signified nothing more than that she was consecrated to the worship of a religion, rival to that which ancient Israel assumed to be "the only true one.[12]

These quotations from Gaines and Dietrick make it obvious that we have only a sketchy, and possibly heavily biased, account of the life of Jezebel that raises more questions than it answers. Furthermore, much that is implicit in the narrative has not been brought to light by commentators, either ancient or modern. Winter has provided an appropriate summing up of the previous discussion. "Jezebel may have been an unsavory character, but she did have a distinction accorded few other women

---

11. Ibid, 23.
12. Stanton, *The Woman's Bible*, II:74–76. See also Nunnally-Cox, *Foremothers*, 87.

in biblical history. She was princess, queen, queen mother, interim ruler of Israel, and grand patroness of the cult and prophets of Baal. The roles of priestess and patroness of Baal would have provided a legitimate basis for her authority and power. This may have been the reason why the authors of the Book of Kings minimized Jezebel's role. She was also a foreigner and a woman, a very powerful woman, and this could only have hurt her memory."[13]

---

13. Winter, *Jezebel*.

22

Athaliah

WE NOW CONSIDER ATHALIAH, the only woman to reign over either Israel or Judah. Her brief story is found in a few verses in 2 Kings, chapters 8 and 11, with parallel accounts in 2 Chronicles, chapters 22-24. She is first mentioned without a name as the daughter of Ahab (red flag!) and as wife of Jehoram, King of Judah (2 Kgs 8:16-18). After Jehoram's death his (and Athaliah's) son Ahaziah reigned for one year over Judah (2 Kgs 8:24-26a). Athaliah's name then appears for the first time, and she is said to be the daughter of Omri, King of Israel (2 Kgs 8:26b). Because she is elsewhere (2 Kgs 8:18) said to be the daughter of Ahab, English translations frequently assume that she was the granddaughter of Omri (who was the father of Ahab).

Upon the death of her son Ahaziah, Athaliah immediately took steps to take control of the throne of Judah. She destroyed all the royal offspring, except for a son of Ahaziah named Joash, who was hidden in the temple for six years by an aunt, the wife of the priest Jehoida (2 Kgs 11:1-3). When Joash was seven years old, Jehoida the high priest, along with the other priests, the Levites, and some of the army commanders, brought out the young Joash, anointed him king and placed the crown on his head (2 Kgs 11:4-11). The people then began to celebrate and say, "Long live the king" (2 Kgs 11:12). When Athaliah heard the commotion she rushed into the temple (where her armed bodyguards could not go) and tore her clothes, crying, "Treason!" "Treason!" (2 Kgs 11:14). Jehoida then commanded her to be brought out of the temple, so that her blood would not defile that holy place, and slain (2 Kgs 11:15-16). Thus ends the life of the only queen to reign over either Israel or Judah.

From this brief account we can see immediately that Athaliah was not popular in the eyes of the Biblical historian (to put it mildly). The last time we see her name in holy writ she is referred to as "the wicked

Athaliah

Athaliah" (2 Chr 24:7). This obviously sums up the attitude of both the author of 1–2 Kings and 1–2 Chronicles toward her. Once again, I suggest that we may need to look at what is *not* said in these texts.

For starters, I raise the question as to how one woman could carry out the killing of all the royal claimants to the throne, as Athaliah is said to have done (2 Kgs 11:1). To imagine that "a mere woman" literally killed all these people strains the bounds of credulity. To accomplish this, she must have had numerous supporters as accomplices. Despite how this appears from our vantage point, what Athaliah did was par for the course in her world. For instance, Solomon had his half brother Adonijah killed when he became a threat to his power. As Brenner has noted, "Nevertheless, because she was a woman and a foreigner who presumed to occupy the Davidic throne, she does not receive the lenient treatment accorded to Solomon who, after all, had behaved similarly."[1] Jehu, when he came to power, wiped out all the descendants of Ahab—and was praised for it by the Biblical writer (cf. 2 Kgs 10:11, 28). Although I make no attempt to justify what Athaliah did, she was certainly no more guilty than some of her male predecessors. And nowhere in the record do we read that Athaliah had some woman killed so she could marry her husband, a la the great King David.

Even more telling than the question of accomplices in the slaughter of the royal claimants to the throne is Athaliah's six-year reign over Judah (1 Kgs 11:3). She is cast in the role of usurper who had no rights to the throne. But how much support must she have had politically, militarily, and religiously to have maintained her throne for that period of time? After all, the usurper Zimri lasted only a week after he took the throne of Israel by force. How much administrative genius must have been required? Even so conservative a commentator as Caldecott has written, "No other woman, before or since, sat upon the throne of David, and it is a proof of her energy and ability that, in spite of her sex, she was able to keep it for six years."[2] Brenner offers a similar conclusion: "Athaliah's reign was considered illegitimate by the biblical narrator—and by the priests, her contemporaries and adversaries—for the following reasons: she was a woman, she was a foreigner, not born to the house of David; she was a Baal worshipper and introduced his cult into Judah as an official alterna-

---

1. Brenner, *The Israelite Woman*, 29.
2. *The International Standard Bible Encyclopaedia*, s.v. "Athaliah."

tive: and she was judged to be bloody and immoral. Let us remember, however, that she did manage to stay in power for six years, despite the religio-political opposition. Her political and organizational skills must have been immense."[3] With Nunnally-Cox we are justified in wondering where the truth of Athaliah and her reign really lies.[4]

---

3. Brenner, *The Israelite Woman*, 31. Cf. also Bellis, *Helpmates Harlots Heroes*, 168–69.
4. Cited in ibid., 168.

23

Huldah

PERHAPS THE MOST REMARKABLE story in the Hebrew Bible of a woman who was independent and clearly not submissive to any man is that of Huldah the prophetess. Her story is contained in 2 Kings 22:14–20, with a parallel account in 2 Chronicles 34:22–28. The setting is near the midpoint of the reign of Josiah, around 621 BCE. One of Josiah's first actions after he came to the throne was to begin a thoroughgoing religious reform (which, by the way, seems to have died with him, since it was only a couple of decades after his death before Judah fell and the Babylonian exile began).

The beginning point of Josiah's reform was the repair of the temple and the reinstitution of the traditional temple worship. During the repair of the temple a book was found (a scroll, actually, in that even the codex form of manuscript that is the forerunner of our books was not yet in use). Those who found the scroll did not know what it was, so they took it to King Josiah and read it in his presence. The exact contents of the scroll are unknown, though most scholars think it was the central section of Deuteronomy, perhaps chapters 12–26 or parts thereof. Josephus, the first-century Jewish historian, says that Eliakim the high priest "lighted upon the holy books of Moses that were laid up in the temple."[1] The word scroll is singular throughout the passage, however, which makes it very unlikely that all the "books of Moses" were found. Several scrolls would have been necessary to contain all five books.

Among the more interesting details that Josephus gives concerning Huldah is his claim that she performed not only a prophetic function but a priestly one as well. He claims that King Josiah sent to her to request that "she would appease God and endeavor to render him propitious to

---

1. *Antiquities* x.iv.ii.

them."² This is the language of priestly sacrifice designed to restore relationships between deities and human beings.

To return to the issue of the scroll found in the course of repairing the temple, there is one thing of which we may be sure, despite our ignorance as to the exact contents of the scroll. It clearly was a passage that spelled out the judgment of God upon disobedience to the law in unmistakable terms. This is made certain by Josiah's response that "great is the wrath of the Lord that burns against us, because our fathers have not listened to the words of this book, to do according to all that is written concerning us" (2 Kgs 22:13b).

After hearing the scroll read, Josiah commanded Hilkiah the high priest and four other men to go and inquire of the Lord as to what the scroll meant for him and the people of Judah. To whom did they go to make this inquiry? For such an important message, contacting the right prophet was imperative. At Josiah's command, Hilkiah went to Huldah and took several men with him to talk with her. In commenting upon this, Nunnally-Cox makes the perceptive comment that "Woman as prophet now appears to be a stationary figure, one accepted by the community and one whose wisdom is sought."³ "Interestingly enough, the high priest did not seek out either the prophet Jeremiah or Zephaniah (though both were probably living at the time [my comment]); he sought the wisdom and prophetic voice of a woman."⁴

An argument hoary with age is that women only became leaders when men failed to take their leadership responsibilities. Evans points to this attitude during the Protestant Reformation. After quoting Calvin's statement that "whenever God wishes to brand man with a mark of ignominy he chooses a woman to prophesy," Evans points out that this might have held true in the time of Deborah (although no evidence in the Biblical text supports this idea), "but in the time of Huldah it is certainly not true, for both Jeremiah and Zephaniah were active at this time. As far as Huldah is concerned, five men who were themselves national leaders went to her without apparent debate, for advice as to the instructions of the Lord concerning the book of the law which Josiah had found. This 'is

---

2. Ibid.
3. Nunnally-Cox, *Foremothers*, 95.
4. Parales, *Hidden Voices*, 24.

Huldah

a strong indication that in this period of Israel's history there was little if any prejudice against a woman uttering a prophecy."[5]

As with most stories of women in the Jewish Scriptures, we know very little about Huldah. She is tersely described as the wife of Shallum, the keeper of the royal wardrobe (2 Kgs 22:14). This would probably indicate that she was not among the poorest classes of Jewish society. "Huldah was obviously a woman of authority, since the king's officials went to consult her, but all that is recorded of her is her one prophetic speech in 2 Kings 22."[6] Huldah is described by one relatively modern author as a prophetess "ranking with Deborah and Hannah."[7] There exists a Jewish tradition that she taught publicly in a school. Another suggests (predictably) that her preaching and teaching were limited to women.[8] The fact that the king and the high priest of Judah felt that she was the one to interpret the word of God at this crisis point in Judah's history says more about her than any mere descriptive words could possibly convey. In this male-dominated, thoroughly patriarchal society, a woman had to interpret Holy Scripture for the king of Judah, the high priest, and three other men of distinction! Brenner both raises the question as to why the king did not seek advice from such men as Jeremiah and Zephaniah, and answers it accordingly: "Perhaps the officials expected that an interview with her would be less embarrassing than one with either of her canonical counterparts; or else Huldah, whose teachings have not been preserved, may have been more respected than her colleagues were during her lifetime. 'We have to remind ourselves that judgments upon personalities and their part in history vary between that of contemporaries and that of posterity.'"[9] In this regard, the words of Parales are worthy of being noted here: "The high priest, the king, and his cabinet apparently put great confidence in what Huldah prophesied to them, because they never questioned anything she said. She told them of the coming judgment, and she identified the book as the Word of God.

---

5. Evans, *Woman in the Bible*, 30–31.

6. McKinlay, *Gendering Wisdom the Host*, 68–69. See also Keener, *Paul, Women & Wives*, 244–45; Rebecca Groothuis, *Good News for Women*, 192–93: Grenze with Kjesbo, *Women in the Church*, 70–71.

7. Deen, *All the Women of the Bible*, 141–42.

8. See *Eerdmans Dictionary of the Bible*, s.v. "Huldah."

9. Brenner, *The Israelite Woman*, 59. See also Bellis, *Helpmates Harlots Heroes*, 175.

"Through this proclamation, Huldah became the first person in the Bible to identify a particular work as the Word of God. This function was later given to men and called 'canonization,' or a process used to identify which writings were Holy Scripture and which were not. Huldah's proclamation to the high priest and king made her the founder of Biblical studies because she authorized God's Word."[10]

Lest one miss the obvious here, the passage that Huldah designated as the Word of God was no minor or peripheral passage, but one that involved nothing less than the destiny of the Jewish nation as it then existed. Bilezikian comments, "Thus, the spiritual leadership of a woman used by God to teach His [sic] will to the king, to the high priest, and to her contemporaries affected the history of the whole nation."[11] Her message was that the judgments contained in the newly discovered scroll were about to be visited upon Judah. Because of his true piety, Josiah would die before this happened, but destruction of Judah was certain.[12] Huldah's prophecy was fulfilled less than forty years later when the Babylonian armies marched against Jerusalem and burned the temple and every "great house" in the city (2 Kgs 25:9).

Elizabeth Cady Stanton, the proto-feminist Biblical scholar, has made some interesting remarks concerning Huldah. "While Huldah was pondering great questions of State and Ecclesiastical Law [sic] her husband was probably arranging the royal buttons and buckles of the household." She goes on to say, "Marriage, in her case, does not appear to have been any obstacle in the way of individual freedom and dignity. She had evidently outgrown the curse of subjection pronounced in the Garden of Eden, as had many other Jewish women."[13] Stanton then goes on to make a telling modern application in these words: "There is a great discrepancy between the character and the conduct of many of the women, and the designs of God as set forth in the Scriptures and enforced by the discipline

---

10. Parales, *Hidden Voices*, 24–25. See also Knowles, *Let Her Be*, 139; Hull, *Equal to Serve*, 112.

11. Bilezikian, *Beyond Sex Roles*, 70.

12. The reference to Josiah's being gathered to his grave in peace (2 Kgs 22:20) has occasioned much discussion, since Josiah died a violent death at the hand of Pharaoh Neco of Egypt. Perhaps we should understand the passage as simply indicating that Josiah would not live to see the prophesied destruction of Judah. For discussion of this issue, see Allen, gen. ed., *I Samuel-Nehemiah*, 286, 417–18; Hubbard & Barker, gen. eds., *2 Kings*, 328: *Mercer Dictionary of the Bible*, s. v. "Huldah," among others.

13. Stanton, *The Woman's Bible*, II:82–83.

of the Church to-day [*sic*]. Imagine the moral hardihood of the reverend gentlemen who should dare to reject such women as Deborah, Huldah and Vashti as delegates to a Methodist conference, and claim the approval of God for such an indignity."[14] One could almost substitute any Christian denomination of today for "Methodist" in Ms. Cady's application. I will not try to add to it or take from it.

From the above discussion one can easily see that the significance of Huldah is far out of proportion to the space she is given in the Jewish Scriptures. The "hermeneutics of suspicion" kicks in once again. Bellis has given voice to that hermeneutics in these words: "It is intriguing to wonder whether Huldah may have prophesied much more than this one instance and whether many of her words have been lost to us. We wish that a book of Huldah had survived."[15] This is a fitting conclusion to the discussion of perhaps the greatest female prophet in the Jewish Scriptures with the possible exception of Deborah.

---

14. Ibid.
15. Bellis, *Helpmates Harlots Heroes*, 175.

24

Noadiah

NOADIAH IS PROBABLY AMONG the least known women of those we have studied so far. Like Vashti and Esther (below), Noadiah belongs to the period when the Jews were subject to Persia. She is mentioned in only one verse of the Jewish Scriptures—Nehemiah 6:14—as one who opposed Nehemiah's rebuilding of the walls of Jerusalem (believing this was too risky and would possibly lead to repercussions from the Persians?). She appears in the text with Tobiah, Sanballat, and "the rest of the prophets." In the Hebrew text of Nehemiah 6:14, Noadiah is described as a *nebiyah* ("prophetess"). The Greek text, interestingly enough, uses the masculine form *prophētēs* ("prophet"). This strongly implies that she fully exercised the prophetic function, as her grouping with "the rest of the prophets" would also indicate. Brenner makes the interesting suggestion that Noadiah was the head of the prophets, and goes on to say, "Noadiah is the only one of the prophets, apart from Shemaiah, who is mentioned by name. This is probably a measure of her importance and political power."[1] Bar-Ilan, on the other hand, says Noadiah was a false prophetess.[2] I surmise that she says this because of Nehemiah's reference to her trying to frighten him. If so, she was part of a larger number of prophets who were doing the same thing, according to the text. Trying to frighten Nehemiah could be understood as making him aware of what the Persians might think or do in response to the rebuilding of the walls of Jerusalem. Warning someone of danger does not equate to being a false prophet! It may have been the case that enemies of Nehemiah and friends as well were trying to warn him about the consequences of his actions in rebuilding the wall. Perhaps Winter has said it best: "Nehemiah had some enemies both within and

---

1. Brenner, *The Israelite Woman*, 60–61.
2. Bar-Ilan, *Some Jewish Women of Antiquity*, 37 n. 21.

outside the prophetic community. Several prophets conspired in a plan to bring him down, but Nehemiah held his ground. We do not know how or why she frightened Nehemiah. It is enough to say that Noadiah was important enough to be remembered and that she made an impact on a man whose book closes the historical section of the Bible."[3]

Murphy lists Noadiah, along with Miriam, Huldah, and the wife of Isaiah, as one of the four women given the title of prophet in the Jewish Scriptures.[4] She goes on to say, "the unremarkable manner in which the Bible mentions the status of these women suggests that the role of prophet was an established one."[5]

Noadiah is otherwise unknown in the Bible. Once more, this silence literally cries out for an explanation. She surely must have spoken out on matters other than the rebuilding of the walls of Jerusalem (although we should note that she is treated no differently from the rest of the prophets in this verse). In all probability a very different picture would emerge if we had her side of the story.

---

3. Winter, *Noadiah*.
4. Why she omits Deborah from the list is mystifying.
5. Murphy, *The Word according to Eve*, 101.

25

Vashti

Vashti was a queen of the Persian Empire whose brief story is told in Esther 1:9–22. Her husband's name is given as Ahasuerus, generally accepted as another name for Xerxes I, who ruled Persia from c. 486–465 BCE. The story begins with an account of the king's showing off the "glories and splendor" (Esth 1:4) of his kingdom for about six months. At the conclusion of this time he then gave a banquet for all the officials and nobles of the 127 provinces of his reign. The banquet lasted for seven days, and on the seventh day the king decided to show yet more of the glories and splendors of his reign—his beautiful queen, Vashti. After seven days of feasting and drinking, the king was apparently in a high state of intoxication (Esth 1:10). In this drunken state he sends seven eunuchs to bring Queen Vashti to him so that he could show her great beauty to the people and the princes of the provinces (Esth 1:11). Just how much of her beauty he wanted to show is an open question. There is a definite ambiguity regarding her being brought "with her royal crown." The Hebrew may with equal plausibility be translated "*in* her royal crown." The latter translation might be seen as implying that she was to wear *only* her crown! In Bellis's words, "The text does not explicitly say that Vashti was to appear only wearing her crown, but it is possible to read the text this way."[1] This would be a very plausible reason for Vashti to refuse the king's order. Be that as it may, the king obviously wanted to put her on display before hundreds of men, most of whom were probably as drunk as he was. Vashti's refusal is probably to be understood as refusing to be made a sex object in the presence of all these men, whatever may be our judgment as to how verse eleven should be translated. As LaCoque comments, "Vashti is treated as a sex object to be displayed or summarily discarded

---

1. Bellis, *Helpmates Harlots Heroes*, 13.

Vashti

when she refuses to comply with an outrageous demand that she play the star of a burlesque."[2]

Obviously Vashti's refusal to come to the king created considerable consternation between him and his advisors, even though some think she was justified by custom, in that women simply did not appear at public feasts.[3] The king quickly called a "cabinet meeting" to discuss what was to be done in the face of Vashti's action. In short order the suggestion came forth that a law should be written that Vashti could never again come before the king, and that her position should be given to one "more worthy than she" (Esth 1:19). The king then issued a decree that every man should be the master of his own house. He had lost it in his house, so he decreed that everyone else should be master of his own house.[4]

Vashti was clearly a person of intelligence and ability. As the king was giving his banquet for the men, she was giving a banquet for all the women in another part of the palace (Esth 1:9). Most of all, she was a woman of courage. As Lucinda Chandler wrote more than a century ago, "Vashti is conspicuous as the first woman recorded whose self-respect and courage enabled her to act contrary to the will of her husband. She was the first 'woman who dared.' . . . She stands for the point in human development when womanliness asserts itself and begins to revolt and to throw off the yoke of sensualism and of tyranny."[5] Her action could easily have resulted in death instead of just being deprived of her position as queen. The words of Berquist are a fitting conclusion to Vashti's story. "She attempted to control her own sexuality and her own life, and she succeeded in asserting how she would act. However, there was a price for her defiance of the king. In gaining her pride, she lost many of her privileges; only she could say if the trade was worthwhile."[6] The biblical text is silent as to the final disposition of Vashti. Since we have no indication of her

---

2. LaCocque, *The Feminine Unconventional*, 51.

3. See, for example, Lofts, *Women in the Old Testament*, 165.

4. This reminds me of a group of men that shall remain nameless who, a few years ago, pontificated that women should all be "graciously submissive" to their husbands. I have heard the suggestion made that they did this because not one of them could accomplish that in his own family!

5. Stanton, *The Woman's Bible*, II:86–87.

6. Berquist, *Reclaiming Her Story*, 156.

being put to death, we might plausibly speculate that she was allowed to continue to live in some remote part of the palace.[7]

---

7. Ibid. Cf. also Stanton, *The Woman's Bible*, II: 90.

26

Esther

THE STORY OF ESTHER follows the story of Vashti both logically and chronologically in the Biblical text. She is the chief character in the remainder of the book of Esther. She is first introduced in the story as a Jewess orphan who is being brought up by her uncle Mordecai. When King Ahasuerus (Xerxes I) deposed Vashti as queen because she refused to be treated as a sex object and be placed on display before all the men of the royal court, the search for a new queen was promptly initiated. The "fairest virgins of all the land" were brought into the royal harem. They were then given a year of beauty treatments. At the end of that year each was given a night in the king's bed, and the one that pleased him most was to be the new queen (Esth 2:14). Her uncle wisely cautioned her to tell no one that she was a Jewess (Esth 2:10). Thus Esther became one of the candidates and eventually succeeded in becoming queen of Persia. Though this may seem degrading and immoral in modern times, in the time of Esther it was an acceptable way of coming into power. "The narrator does not intimate that Esther should be condemned for her willingness to try out for the position of queen. In addition, oppressed people often must use whatever means are available to them to survive."[1]

Mordecai continued to station himself at the gate of the palace in order to keep up with what was happening with Esther. Enter the villain! A man named Haman came to hate Mordecai because the latter would not recognize his high status by bowing down to him. The text is silent as to the reason Mordecai refused to honor Haman. Perhaps to a pious Jew the kind of obeisance to which Haman was accustomed smacked of divine honors, something that should not be paid to mere humans.[2]

---

1. Bellis, *Helpmates Harlots Heroes*, 213.
2. Berquist posits this as the reason, while admitting that the text is completely silent

As Lofts comments, "Fawning courtiers, each seeking to outstrip the others in adulation, had forced the prestige of royalty so high that there was no clear line between it and divinity."[3]

A fairly ancient, but poorly supported, theory is that Haman was an Amalekite, one of the ancient enemies of Israel.[4] Apparently the theory is based solely on the reference to Haman as son of Hammedatha the Agagite (Esth 3:1). Agag was king of the Amalekites during the reign of Saul and was slain by the prophet/judge Samuel (1 Sam 15:9, 32–33). Since a gap of more than five hundred years intervened between Saul and the reign of Ahasuerus, to assume that "Agagite" and "Amalekite" are to be equated is hazardous, to say the least. Having said this, LaCocque has made a very plausible case for a typological comparison of Saul/Agag and Haman/Mordecai.[5]

Regardless of the source of Mordecai's attitude toward Haman, the latter conceived a master plan of retaliation. He would have all the Jews in the whole kingdom of Persia exterminated! Mordecai learned of the plot and reported it to Esther. Despite the death penalty prescribed for anyone who came into the king's presence without being summoned, Esther dared to approach him with her request. She coyly refused to divulge what she wanted at first, and invited the king and Haman to a banquet. Haman took this to be a great honor, because he was the only guest of the king and queen, and especially when Esther invited them back for a second banquet the following day. She promised that, at the second banquet, she would make her request known to the king.

In the meantime Haman, at the urging of his wife, had a gallows constructed that was seventy-five-feet high, with the intention of hanging Mordecai from it (Esth 5:14). But, to his dismay, at the banquet on the second day Esther revealed to the king that Haman was the source of the plot to exterminate all her people. The king then decreed that Haman be hanged on the gallows he had had built for Mordecai. (I can't resist the comment that Haman was neither the first nor the last to be hanged on the gallows he or she had prepared for someone else!)

---

on this issue. Berquist, *Reclaiming Her Story*, 159. See also Day, *Gender and Difference*, 169.

3. Lofts, *Women in the Old Testament*, 173.
4. Ibid., 170; *The International Standard Bible Encyclopaedia*, s.v. "Haman."
5. LaCocque, *The Feminine Unconventional*, 65–83.

Esther

In the Persian Empire, when an edict was made law it could not be changed. Ahasuerus could not simply revoke the edict designed to exterminate the Jews, even though he realized he had been tricked into signing it; so he did the next best thing. He issued another edict saying the Jews could gather together, arm themselves, and destroy those who were sent out to destroy them (Esth 8:11).

Once again, one could read this story in such a way that Esther appears to be the perfect submissive woman. A closer examination of the text, however, shows the superficiality of this view. When she learned of the plot to exterminate her and her people, she risked her life by going in to see the king. (According to Josephus the throne was surrounded by men with axes, ready to punish anyone that came into the king's presence without being summoned.[6]) Before going in to the king she sent *orders* to Mordecai to assemble all the Jews living in Susa (including the males, quite obviously) and to fast for three days, after which she would go in to see the king (Esth 4:15).[7] No great intelligence is required to see that Esther was in control of events from that moment on. *She* invited the king and Haman to a banquet. *She* exposed Haman's plot to the king—and later succeeded in getting a new law passed that allowed the Jews to arm themselves and slay their enemies. Although "Esther was of an alien culture, which she concealed from the king, and [*sic*] when the very existence of her people was threatened, she intervened to save them and herself from extinction. She moved from naïve, unassuming passivity to cunning, daring, and courageous action."[8] LaCocque aptly sums up her story in these words: "So both stories (Judith[9] and Esther) tell about the rise of powerless females to a position of power in a strongly male-dominated world."[10] I will now turn attention to some key female figures in the Christian Testament.

---

6. *Antiquities* xi.vi.3.
7. Cf. Day, *Gender and Difference*, 170.
8. Winter, *Esther*.
9. A book in the Roman Catholic canon which is not accepted as canonical by many other Christians.
10. LaCocque, *The Feminine Unconventional*, 72.

27

Anna

THE EARLIEST NAME OF a woman who is called a prophet in the Christian Testament appears in the second chapter of Luke. There Anna is described as continually present in the temple, serving God night and day with fastings and prayers. This description comes at the point when Jesus was brought as an infant to the temple to complete the requirements of the Mosaic law. According to the text Anna had been married for seven years, and then had lived as a widow for eighty-four years. As Getty-Sullivan has noted, the text is unclear as to whether the eighty-four years represents her age, or a period after the death of her husband.[1] Bauckham suggests that we should read these numbers as seven plus eighty-four, and that "Luke" has deliberately schematized Anna's life in multiples of the ancient perfect number seven: "two weeks of years before marriage, one week of years married, twelve weeks of years as a widow."[2] I think Bauckham may very well be correct, but to pursue that issue goes beyond the purposes of this study.

Anna is also said to have been of the tribe of Asher, which, according to Jewish tradition, was noted for its beautiful and talented women who, because of these qualities, were qualified for royal and high priestly marriage.[3] Anna is the Christian Testament equivalent of the name Hannah in the Jewish Scriptures. Her name, her father's name, and her tribe probably all had theological overtones to the author of Luke.[4]

1. Getty-Sullivan, *Women in the New Testament*, 38.
2. Bauckham, *Gospel Women*, 99.
3. *International Standard Bible Encyclopaedia*, s.v. "Anna."
4. See Getty-Sullivan, *Women in the New Testament*, 35–41 for suggestions along this line. For a thorough discussion of the significance of Anna's being from the tribe of Asher and the schematization of her life in periods of seven years see Bauckham, *Gospel Women*, 77–101.

Anna

Also serving in the temple was an aged priest by the name of Simeon. Anna's placement alongside Simeon would appear to be a very intentional action on the part of the author. N. M. Flanagan has found no less than thirteen man-woman stories in the Gospel of Luke.[5] As Spencer points out, these two alone recognize in the infant Jesus the savior of Jew and Gentile.[6] As a careful analysis of the text will show, their roles were parallel, not vertical. One of the stronger clues supporting this parallel status is simply the word *prophētis* ("prophetess"). We have previously seen this term applied to Miriam, Deborah, Huldah, and Noadiah in the Jewish Scriptures. Only one other woman in the Jewish Scriptures receives this title, the wife of Isaiah (Isa 8:3). Many have interpreted the word "prophetess" in that text as referring solely to her status as the wife of a prophet.[7] Watts counters this interpretation, saying, "Rather it is understood that she, like Hulda [sic] (2 Kgs 22:14) served as a prophet in the Temple as well as participating in the sign by birthing a son."[8] (Isaiah's wife will be discussed later in the section on unnamed women of the Bible.)

To return to the story of Anna, we are told that when she was confronted with the infant Jesus she continued to speak of him "to all (not just the women!) those who were looking for the redemption of Jerusalem, that the day of their spiritual deliverance had come."[9] The tense of the verbs used of Anna in Luke 2:38 suggests an ongoing, continuous witness to Jesus on the part of Anna. As Cunningham and Hamilton have pointed out, "This wasn't a quiet word behind the scenes, but was a public proclamation in the central place of worship. In fact, it was a defining moment in Christian history."[10] In Deen's words, she (Anna) "stands foremost among prophetesses in the New Testament."[11]

Many interpreters have tried to limit Anna's service in the temple to praying and fasting, that is, the service of worship.[12] Deen suggests that

---

5. Cited in Hubbard & Barker, gen. eds., *Luke 1–9:20*, 122.

6. Aida Besancon Spencer, *Beyond the Curse*, 104. Cf. also Edersheim, *The Life and Times of Jesus the Messiah*, 201.

7. Examples are found in Hubbard & Barker, gen. eds., *Isaiah 1–33*, 113; Deen, *All the Women of the Bible*, 141–42

8. Hubbard & Barker, 113.

9. *International Standard Bible Encyclopaedia*, s.v. "Anna."

10. Cunningham, Hamilton, & Rogers, *Why Not Women?* 57.

11. Deen, *All the Women of the Bible*, 173.

12. For example, Summers, 41; Hubbard & Barker, gen. eds., *Luke 1–9:20*, 122–23; Barclay, 23.

"Probably she held the place in the Temple of a deaconess or Sister of Charity."[13] Although we have no evidence of such functions in the Jewish temple, Deen may well be on the right track in suggesting that the service Anna rendered went beyond the service of worship and included some sort of official position. The Greek verb for Anna's service is *latreuō*. Of its twenty usages in the Christian Testament outside of the present passage, it is used of one's total service to God six times.[14] In six other cases it is ambiguous, but seems to include worship and other service as well.[15] Four times the same word is used of priestly service.[16] Only four times is it unambiguously limited to the service of worship.[17] Therefore, since 80 percent of the usages of this verb in the New Testament include more than the service of worship, to limit its meaning to worship in Luke 2:37 is a highly questionable interpretation.

---

13. Deen, *All the Women of the Bible*, 173.
14. Matt 4:10, Luke 1:74, Acts 24:14, 27:23; Rom 1:9, 2 Tim 1:3.
15. Luke 4:8, Acts 7:7, 26:7; Phil 3:3, Heb 9:14, 12:28.
16. Heb 8:5, 9:9, 10:2, 13:10.
17. Acts 7:42, Rom 1:25, Rev 7:15, 22:3.

28

Mary, Mother of Jesus

For the purposes of this study of Mary, I will primarily limit my discussion to one passage in the second chapter of the Gospel of John. It is a familiar story to many. Jesus attends a wedding in Cana of Galilee. The host runs out of wine, and Jesus's mother informs him of the situation. After a cryptic question to his mother, Jesus turns water into wine, the best that the wedding party has tasted.

As we begin to look at the story, I would first like to call attention to the absence of Joseph. The last we hear of him is in the story of Jesus being taken to the temple at Jerusalem when he was twelve years old. Presumably Joseph died sometime between that story and the time Jesus began his earthly ministry. This may have meant that Mary had been in charge of the family for several years. (Perhaps it is worth noting that even in the story of Jesus's being taken to the temple at age twelve, Joseph is the silent partner. Mary is the one who confronts Jesus over his actions. Neither here nor in the account of his being brought to the temple when he was eight days old does Joseph speak. Hence it *could* be the case that Mary took charge of the family even while Joseph was alive.) Be this as it may, she is quick to take control of the situation at the wedding.

Let me confess at the outset that this story raises more questions than it answers. To begin with, why did Mary confront Jesus as she did? We have traditionally been led to believe that she knew his power, and that he would perform a miracle so the host would suffer no embarrassment. Obviously this could have been the case, though I personally think it is very unlikely. We have no solid evidence that any members of Jesus's human family believed in him as other than a human being until after the resurrection, contrary to the story of the angelic announcement of Jesus's birth in the first chapter of Luke.¹ In fact, in Mark we find a situation in which Jesus's human family seems to have thought he had gone crazy, and perhaps wanted to take him home so that he did not embarrass the family any further (see Mark 3:21–35).²

Many scholars of the Christian Testament today see the birth stories as late additions to the Gospels, and hence perhaps more theological than merely historical. This would mean late first century theology injected back into the time of Jesus's birth. One fact that points in this direction is that Mark, the earliest Gospel, does not contain a birth story.³

The easiest way to get a feel for the lateness of these stories is to read the stories in Luke 1 and compare them with the episode in Luke 2 where Jesus was taken to the temple at age twelve. When Mary and Joseph started home after Passover, they had gone a day's journey before realizing that Jesus was not with them. They returned to Jerusalem and found him in the temple, conversing with teachers. Notice Mary's response. She said to him, "Son, why have you treated us this way? Behold, your father and I have been anxiously looking for you" (Luke 2:48b). This doesn't sound to me as though Mary knew she was talking to the Lord! It sounds much more like an ordinary worried mother whose twelve-year-old son has gotten separated from her.

Lest I get too far afield, let me return to the text and the issue as to why Mary confronted Jesus as she did. Although most English translations make it appear that Jesus and the disciples were invited to the wedding, that is not necessarily the case. The verb "invited" in verse two is singular. Literally translated, the verse reads, "and Jesus also was invited and his disciples to the wedding." This could mean that both Jesus and his disciples were invited to the wedding. It could also mean that Jesus was invited, and the disciples tagged along! (Omission of a verb is fairly common in Greek, so reading this "Jesus was invited and the disciples [came] to the wedding" would not be unusual.) If we imagine a small wedding celebration of perhaps twenty or thirty people (as would be probable in a

---

1. For a contra argument that Jesus's mother represents the ideal faithful disciple in the Fourth Gospel, see F. Scott Spencer, *Dancing Girls*, 86–87.

2. Cf. Swidler, *Biblical Affirmations of Woman*, 117.

3. There is a small, but very vocal, contingent of New Testament scholars who do not accept Mark as the earliest of the Gospels to be written. I believe that I am correct in maintaining that the majority support the idea that Mark was the earliest of the Gospels to be written.

small village like Cana), what would have likely happened if twelve extra people showed up? If you haven't picked up on where this is going, I am suggesting that Jesus's mother *may* have held him responsible for the situation because he had brought his disciples along.

This brings us to the cryptic response of Jesus: "And Jesus said to her, 'Woman, what do I have to do with you? My hour has not yet come'" (John 2:4). The question contains only five words in the Greek text. Literally translated, the question is, "What to me and to you, woman?"[4] A comparison of English translations reveals that this has been interpreted primarily in two ways. One approach sees it is a question as to what business it is of Jesus or his mother that they have run out of wine. The other sees it as a question as to the relationship of Mary and Jesus, that is, "Woman, do you really understand what our true relationship is?" I am inclined to the latter understanding, in view of Jesus's statement that his hour had not yet come, and the revelation in John 17:1 that Jesus's "hour" was the hour of his crucifixion.

If we read John 2 without the "filter" of Luke 1:1–20, what do we find? Without any dogmatism whatever I suggest that we find a woman without a husband who is head of her family. Mary has five sons and an unspecified number of daughters (see Mark 6:3, cf. Matt 13:55–56). She, for whatever reasons, held her eldest son responsible for a situation that was potentially a major embarrassment for the host. (Few things could be more embarrassing in the eastern world than to have insufficient food or drink on a festive occasion such as a wedding.) Mary does not hesitate to challenge this son by making him aware of the situation. His response to her either means that the situation is none of their business, or that Mary needs to reconsider what her true relationship to him really is. When Mary instructs the servants to do whatever Jesus tells them to do, she may have done so because she knew that his miraculous powers could alleviate the situation (although we may question whether Jesus yet has a reputation for doing miracles or not, because in John, at least, this is the first miracle Jesus performs), or it may have meant nothing more than that the situation was Jesus's responsibility, and she expected him to take care of it. Regardless of how we read the text, Mary emerges as an independent woman who is not controlled by her eldest son or any other male.

---

4. Cf. F. Scott Spencer, *Dancing Girls*, 86.

29

Mary Magdalene

MARY MAGDALENE IS MENTIONED in four contexts in the Gospels. She is listed in Luke 8:1–3 as one of the women who went around with Jesus and supported him out of her private means. The only other information we get in this passage is that seven demons had gone out of her (Luke 8:2). Second, she is mentioned as one of the women who was at the cross when Jesus was crucified (after all the male disciples had forsaken him, according to Mark 14:50). Third, she is mentioned as one of the women who was at the tomb when Jesus was buried (Mark 15:47). Finally, she is mentioned as coming to the tomb on Sunday after the crucifixion and finding it empty.[1] MacHaffie and others have noted that the name of Mary Magdalene appears first in all the lists of the women present at Jesus's death, burial, and the empty tomb. She goes on to say, "A strong tradition that claimed that Jesus first appeared to Mary probably existed in the early churches"[2] (despite the omission of this in Paul's account of the post-resurrection appearances of Jesus in 1 Corinthians 15:5–8).

While the other three Gospels mention other women besides Mary Magdalene going to the empty tomb of Jesus, the Gospel of John mentions her alone (although the phrase "*we* do not know where they have laid Him" [emphasis mine] in verse two implies the presence of others, perhaps the other women mentioned in the other three Gospels). Despite differences among these other Gospels, Mary Magdalene remains the constant in all three. Not only so, but her name is always mentioned first

---

1. I will not attempt to untangle the knotty problem as to the number or the names of the women who found the empty tomb. The reader is invited to compare Mark 16:1 with Matthew 28:1, Luke 24:1–12, and John 20:1.

2. MacHaffie, *Her Story*, 18.

Mary Magdalene

in the accounts, a fact of no small significance in trying to evaluate the character and significance of this woman.[3]

Through the years, Mary Magdalene has suffered confusion with the other Marys in the Gospels. Weems argues that there are no less than seven women by that name who are mentioned in the Gospels.[4] Part of the confusion has stemmed from the anointing stories (see below). The Fourth Gospel's naming of Mary of Bethany as the woman who anointed Jesus has been combined with the "woman who was a sinner" in Luke's account and the reference to seven demons having gone out of Mary Magdalene.[5] This is quite a composite picture, to say the least![6] Further, the "woman who was a sinner" has been taken as indicating she was a prostitute, and this has been transferred to Mary Magdalene. Prostitution is hardly the only sin of which a woman (or man) could be guilty, and even in Luke, the only Gospel who refers to the anointing woman as a sinner, identifying the woman as a prostitute is pure speculation. There is nothing in the texts to support the theory that Mary Magdalene was the woman who anointed Jesus, or that she was a prostitute. In Getty-Sullivan's words, "Nowhere in the Gospels is Mary Magdalene referred to as a sinner, still less a prostitute."[7] As far as her lifestyle is concerned, the reference to seven demons having gone out of her is all that we have. Murphy reflects a concise picture of the layers of interpretation foisted upon Mary Magdalene in the following words: "The Mary Magdalene of legend is one of the more remarkable phenomena deriving from Scripture, her reputation and symbolism in subsequent ages held up by a rickety scaffolding of interpretation erected upon a meager foundation of text. Her career—follower of Jesus, witness to the crucifixion and burial of Jesus, first among the disciples to see the empty tomb, reputed prostitute, presumed rival of the apostle Peter, exemplar both of lust and of

---

3. Cf. de Boer, *Mary Magdalene*, 45.

4. Weems, *Just a Sister Away*, 88.

5. This confusion apparently goes back as far as Tertullian in the late second century CE. Cf. Knowles, *Let Her Be*, 59.

6. For a concise statement of the fallacious reasoning that has led to the conclusion that Mary Magdalene was a prostitute; see de Boer, Mary Magdalene, 11. For a fuller discussion, including the positive treatment of Mary Magdalene in Gnostic writings, see Schaberg, "Before Mary: The Ancestresses of Jesus," 13–23, Trible, et al., *Feminist Approaches*, 75–89.

7. Getty-Sullivan, *Women in the New Testament*, 183.

the power of repentance—comes readily to mind when feminist biblical scholars consider the fate of Scripture in the hands of men."[8]

Although scholars down through the centuries have occasionally challenged the equating of Mary Magdalene with the "woman who was a sinner" in Luke and the sister of Martha of Bethany, official Christendom has been very slow to acknowledge any validity to such a challenge. For example, when a sixteenth-century French Biblical scholar argued for these as three separate women, his teaching was promptly condemned by the church as "dangerous."[9]

The last decade or so has witnessed a virtual explosion of scholarly, and not so scholarly, writings about Mary Magdalene, which I will make no attempt to assess or even summarize.[10] I will limit my focus to what we have in the four Gospels.

First of all, the meager information we have in the Gospels reflects a woman who is independent and not defined by any male such as a husband or father (unless one should choose to argue that she was defined by Jesus). She is a woman of independent financial means (whether from inheritance or, as traditionally suggested, from her work as a prostitute) who supported the ministry of Jesus and his other disciples. Second, she is depicted as a woman who was seriously impaired in her ability to function normally and who was healed of her impairment by Jesus. (In the world of Jesus, if a person could not function normally the inability was usually attributed to demons.)[11] Because the number seven is the universal number of completeness, the severity of her plight is magnified.[12] She was thought to have been under the *complete* power of evil forces. Her healing was probably a major factor in her becoming a follower of Jesus, though the text does not mention this in any specific way.[13] This sums up all we know of Mary Magdalene from the Gospels.[14]

---

8. Murphy, *The Word According to Eve*, 196.

9. See de Boer, *Mary Magdalene*, 9.

10. For those who might wish to pursue a more in-depth study of Mary Magdalene, an excellent starting point would be de Boer, *Mary Magdalene*, and the sources she cites.

11. See Weems, *Just a Sister Away*, 89–91.

12. Cf. Dornisch, *A Woman Reads the Gospel of Luke*, 184.

13. For a discussion as to how her place of origin (Magdala) may have made her responsive to the teachings of Jesus, see de Boer, *Mary Magdalene*, 40–41, and Weems, *Just a Sister Away*, 88–89.

14. Cf. Knowles, *Let Her Be*, 158.

Mary Magdalene

Next I will focus on the ways in which this woman broke out of the role of women as defined by her society. To begin with the obvious, Mary Magdalene's decision to follow Jesus and the male disciples from place to place would have taken a great deal of courage. Women were not supposed to be seen publicly in the company of men or to engage in public conversation with men (cf. the story of Jesus's conversation with the Samaritan woman in John 4:7-27 and the reaction of the disciples).[15] By this action she risked being seen as a prostitute, regardless of what the facts may have been. As Parales notes, "Not only did Mary Magdalene support Jesus and the disciples, she and the other women courageously followed Jesus around the countryside. Certainly such audacious behavior, following about after a company of men, could have brought judgment on their heads, especially because they had to leave their homes and families to do so. Nowhere were these women shown to need a man for anything, even though they lived in a culture that regarded women as inferior to, and dependent upon, males."[16]

As already noted, we have no real evidence that Mary Magdalene was a prostitute. As Kraemer and D'Angelo have noted, "Feminist interpretation has debunked the image of the fallen and repentant Magdalene, substituting the figure of Mary Magdalene as the intrepid and faithful disciple of Jesus, an apostle with and to the twelve and a witness to the resurrection."[17] (See below.)

Mary Magdalene's greatest claim to fame comes from the account of the empty tomb. I will limit my comments here to the account in John 20:1-18. There we are told that she came to the tomb of Jesus and found the stone rolled away and the tomb empty. Her immediate response was to run to Peter and the mysterious "disciple whom Jesus loved"[18] and report what she had found. They went to the tomb, where Peter entered and found the linen wrappings and face cloth in which Jesus was buried (John

---

15. Cf. Weems, *Just a Sister Away*, 87.
16. Parales, *Hidden Voices*, 34-35.
17. Kraemer & D'Angelo, eds., *Women & Christian Origins*, 105.
18. Some have even argued that this mysterious disciple was none other than Mary Magdalene. This is but one among many attempts to identify the "disciple whom Jesus loved." Probably this is based upon the non-canonical *Gospel of Mary*, which features her as the "beloved disciple." Cf. Kraemer & D'Angelo, eds., *Women & Christian Origins*, 341. For a more detailed discussion of the identity of the beloved disciple, see Grassi, *The Secret Identity of the Beloved Disciple*.

20:6–7). The other disciple looked in and "saw and believed" (John 20:8). Interestingly these two disciples returned home, apparently telling no one what they had observed (John 20:9). Mary, on the other hand remained at the tomb. When she looked into the tomb, instead of finding the wrappings and face cloth as had the two male disciples, she saw two angels who questioned why she was weeping.[19] She answered, "Because they have taken away my Lord, and I do not know where they have laid him" (John 20:11–13). At this point Jesus himself appeared, but she did not recognize him until he called her by name (John 20:16). For the reader of this Gospel this identifies her as one of the "sheep" who hear and respond to the voice of the shepherd (John 10:27). Jesus then commissioned Mary to go to the male disciples and tell them of his imminent ascension to his father (John 20:17). She immediately went to the disciples, telling them she had seen the Lord (alive) and what he had said to her. This earned her the title in later tradition of "apostle to the apostles."[20] We might further note that a constant feature of all four Gospels is that women are commissioned to report Jesus's resurrection to the male disciples.[21] The words of Scanzoni and Hardesty are worthy of being quoted here at some length:

> Jesus appeared first not to Peter, the "vicar" of the church, nor even to John, the "beloved." Women were the first to receive the central fact of the gospel and the first to be instructed to tell it abroad....
>
> Thus Jesus' life on earth from beginning to end outlines a paradigm for women's place. His actions upset and appalled his contemporaries, dumbfounded his critics, and flabbergasted his male disciples. Since that day the church has struggled, if sometimes unenthusiastically and unsuccessfully, to cut through the barbed wire of cultural custom and taboo in order to emulate the

---

19. We have a slight overtone here of Luke's account of the women at the tomb, although in that Gospel the women encounter two men in dazzling apparel (Luke 24:4). In Mark the women encounter a young man (Mark 16:5) and in Matthew they encounter an angel (Matt 28:2). In the Fourth Gospel we appear to have a conflation of the tradition of an angel in Matthew and the two men in Luke.

20. Cf. F. Scott Spencer, *Dancing Girls*, 96; Swidler, *Biblical Affirmations of Woman*, 204; Eisen, *Women Officeholders in Early Christianity*, 51; Fiorenza, *Sharing Her Word*, 114.

21. In a way, Luke is an exception to this statement, in that the women seem to go of their own accord and report what they have seen to the other disciples. Since the other three Gospels report the commissioning of the women by the "angel(s)" at the tomb, this could be an early attempt to avoid the specter of female apostles. It could also be nothing more than an accident of transmission during the oral period of the Gospel traditions.

Mary Magdalene

One who promised both women and men that they could be "free indeed."[22]

What does this all have to say to those who would deny women the opportunity to serve as preachers or teachers today?

---

22. Scanzoni & Hardesty, *All We're Meant to Be*, 81.

30

Martha and Mary of Bethany

THE STORY OF THESE two sisters appears in Luke 10:38–42 and John 11:1—12:8. They had a brother named Lazarus, and Jesus is said explicitly to have loved Martha, her sister, and Lazarus (John 11:5). No father is mentioned, so we do not know whether he was alive at this point or not. Based on the stories in all four gospels of a woman anointing Jesus with expensive ointment or perfume, many conjectures have been made. In Mark and Matthew the anointing is by an unnamed woman and takes place at Bethany in the house of Simon the leper (Mark 14:3–8, cf. Matt 26:6–13). Bethany was also the place where Martha, Mary, and Lazarus lived (John 11:10). Hence some have argued that Simon the leper was the father of Mary, Martha, and Lazarus. In Luke the anointing is also by an unnamed woman and takes place in an unnamed Pharisee's house at an unnamed location (Luke 7:36–50). Only in John is the woman who anointed Jesus identified as Mary of Bethany.

Taking all four accounts as variants of the same story would require equating the unnamed Pharisee in Luke's version with Simon the leper in Matthew and Mark. Only by this circuitous sort of reasoning can one get the father of Martha, Mary, and Lazarus into the picture. These anointing stories present a number of difficulties in interpretation, and it is perhaps best just to admit that we do know who the father of Martha, Mary, and Lazarus was.[1]

To return to the story of the sisters, I will first focus upon Luke 10:38–42. Here Jesus is welcomed into the house by Martha. According to the custom of the day, the man of the house should have done the welcoming. Neither Lazarus nor the father of the sisters is mentioned. In

---

1. For a thorough discussion of the anointing stories see Albright and Freedman, gen. eds., *The Gospel according to John I-XII*, 449–54.

fact, outside the Gospel of John the name Lazarus appears only at Luke 16 as the name of a poor beggar in Jesus's parable. There is no apparent connection between this poor beggar and Lazarus of Bethany. Any connection is mere speculation. All this would seem to place Martha in the unusual position of head of the household who welcomes a distinguished guest. She is probably the older of the two sisters, in that she is mentioned first and is said to have had a sister called Mary (Luke 7:39). We should also note the reference to Martha's welcoming Jesus into *her* house (Luke 10:38). The Greek manuscripts vary considerably in the contents of Luke 10:38, with perhaps the strongest evidence favoring either the reading "into the house" or "into her house," both of which could be taken to mean that it was in fact Martha's house. The possessive "her" is supported by the KJV, Amplified Bible, Rheims New Testament, NASB, NIV, and NRSV, among others. Some have argued that this is a matter of little significance. Ray Summers, for example, says, "The use of the word *her* has led some interpreters to think that it was Martha's house and that her sister Mary, and her brother Lazarus lived there. This cannot be demonstrated and is of relatively little importance."[2] I respectfully disagree with my former professor—a woman in the role of head of a household at this point in history is, in my judgment, a matter of considerable significance.

As the story continues, we read that Martha was busily involved in preparing a meal for their distinguished guest. "Mary, however, took the supposedly male role: she 'sat at the Lord's feet and listened to his teaching.'"[3] Much more is involved in this scene than meets the eye. "Sitting at the feet" was a technical term for learning the law from a rabbi. As Tolbert notes, "To sit at a person's feet was the idiom equivalent to our expression 'to study under someone' (cf. Acts 22:3). So Mary is pictured as a student, in itself a revolutionary innovation, for rabbis did not teach women."[4] In Swidler's words, "Martha took the woman's typical role and 'was distracted with much serving.'"[5] Knowles makes the point that Martha was *distracted*, not *overburdened*, and suggests that another message is hidden in her words. He goes on to quote Kenneth E. Bailey's suggestion as to what a "cultural insider" of that time would have heard:

2. Summers, *Commentary on Luke*, 137.

3. Swidler, 192. *Biblical Affirmations of Woman*, 192. Cf. Thurston, *Knowing Her Place*, 15.

4. Allen, gen. ed., *Luke-John*, 95.

5. Swidler, *Biblical Affirmations of Woman*, 192.

Biblical Women—Submissive?

"The other rabbis don't have women disciples! What's happening under my nose is outrageous and unprecedented! What will the neighbors think and what will the local rabbis say? Imagine—my sister—a disciple of a rabbi! If she continues she will be involved in daily interaction with *young unmarried* men! Who will marry the poor girl after this? Her reputation will be ruined! She'll listen to you, Jesus! You *must* tell her that her place is here in the kitchen with me!"[6] This probably captures the essence of public opinion on the matter of women studying under rabbis. Sayers has written, no doubt with tongue in cheek, "For Martha was doing a really feminine job, whereas Mary was just behaving like any other disciple, male or female; and that is a hard pill to swallow."[7] In the world of Jesus, women were not considered worthy of learning the law. In fact, we have evidence of very extreme opposition to teaching the law to women on the part of some rabbis. Swidler cites a couple of prime examples from the first-century rabbi Eliezer: "Rather should the Torah be burned than entrusted to a woman....Whoever teaches his daughter the Torah is like one who teaches her obscenity."[8]

The Synoptic Gospels rather consistently show Jesus's disciples as somewhat dull and slow to understand the true nature of his person and work. By contrast, "In reporting Mary's anointing of Jesus at Bethany, the Evangelists [*sic*] imply that Mary understood the true nature of Jesus's messiahship, a theological insight that Jesus's male disciples failed to grasp throughout his entire earthly ministry. This female follower seemed to realize that her Lord's vocation included death. On this basis, Jesus rebuked the disciples' grumbling against her, and he praised her action."[9]

Despite Martha's failure to understand the goodness of Mary's relationship to Jesus, Martha did, on another occasion, demonstrate an understanding of Jesus that was superior to most of his male disciples. Echoing Peter's words in the Synoptic Gospels (Mark 8:29; Matt 16:16; Luke 9:20) she says, "I have believed that you are the Christ, the Son of God, *even* He who comes into the world" (John 11:27).

Much has been made by interpreters of the supposed contrast between Mary's "better part" and Martha's domestic serving. Actually the

---

6. Knowles, *Let Her Be*, 56.

7. Sayers, *Are Women Human*, 46–47.

8. Swidler, *Biblical Affirmations of Woman*, 154. For an assessment of this passage and a very different conclusion by Adele Reinhartz, see Levine, ed., *Women like this*, 163–72.

9. Grenz with Muirkjesbo, *Women in the Church*, 76.

text says nothing about a "better part." (Notwithstanding the number of English translations that contain this phrase.) The text reads, "Mary has chosen the *good* (*tēn agathē*) part which shall not be taken from her." There is no comparison between what Mary does and what Martha does in the text itself. *What* Martha does is not the issue. The issue is that she was "distracted with all her preparations." Like many "Marthas" down through the centuries, she was trying to do too much by way of preparation for an honored guest. The "many things" that distracted Martha were probably many dishes of food. I think we need to hear Jesus's reply in this fashion: "Martha, you're trying to cook up a seven course meal, when all any one of us needs is a bowl of soup!" To read this text as saying that "spiritual concerns" are more important than other types of service is to impose on the text an interpretation that is alien to it.[10]

The story of Martha and Mary is typical of "Luke's" tendency to show women in roles normally reserved for men. While I am sensitive to the feminist scholars who note that the women are mostly silenced in this Gospel,[11] at least they are present in ways not mentioned by the other Gospels. Both women are shown acting without direction or control of any male. From this text one would not know that they had either a father or a brother. Only in the Fourth Gospel do we have the information that they had a brother named Lazarus. He is totally absent from this story in Luke.

A detail of this story that had eluded me until very recently may have a great deal to say about these two sisters. In John 11:1 Bethany is depicted as "the village of Mary and her sister Martha." Obviously, this could be read as meaning only that it was the village where Mary and Martha lived. I would hazard the guess, however, that if the reference had been to Bethany as the village of Lazarus and his father, it would be assumed that they were leaders of the village. To interpret this text as meaning that Mary and Martha were leaders of the village is at least as plausible as any other reading. The treatment of Martha and Mary in later Christian tradition fairly well reverses the traditional idea that Mary is the one who chose the better part. In that tradition Martha is depicted as strong, confident, and industrious,

---

10. For an excellent discussion of this supposed contrast, see Thurston, *Knowing Her Place*, 10–16. For arguments that the story is not really about two historical women, but about problems in the church at the time the Gospel of Luke was written, see Getty-Sullivan, *Women in the New Testament*, 191–98.

11. See, for example, F. Scott Spencer, *Dancing Girls*, 144–60.

whereas Mary is placed in the shadow of Martha. When we move from the Gospel of Luke to that of John, this reversal may already be apparent. As Moltmann-Wendel notes, "John throws overboard our traditional Christian image of Martha: he restores to life the aggressive, disturbing, sage, active Martha who went against all the conventions: mistress of the house, housewife, apostle, the woman who stands beside Peter in her own right." She further notes how Martha's confession in John 11:27 resembles Peter's confession of Jesus in the Synoptic Gospels.[12] In later tradition a legend developed that parallels the well-known story of St. George slaying the dragon. In this tradition Martha became the dragon-slayer (an eminently masculine role!), as depicted in numerous art works in the Middle Ages.[13] This picture of Martha has been largely forgotten, while the picture of the busy housewife who is too busy to listen to Jesus's teachings like her sister has survived.

---

12. Moltmann-Wendel, *The Women around Jesus* (in German), 24–26.
13. For two examples, see ibid., 16, 41.

31

Mary, Mother of John Mark

This Mary is mentioned in the New Testament only at Acts 12:12. She was probably widowed at this point, in that the house mentioned in the verse is her house. She must have been a woman of considerable means, because the text tells us that *many* were gathered in her house for prayer. Another argument that Mary was a woman of some wealth is that her household included servants.[1] Others, however, have pointed out that the slave status of the damsel Rhoda did not necessarily identify her as a slave in Mary's household. Reimer, for example, says "In Mary's house there is a *paidiskē* a 'slave woman.' The text does not say that Mary is her owner. If she was Mary's slave, opening the door may have been one of her tasks, but it need not have been her sole occupation. . . .The slave woman Rhoda behaves as if she were not a slave. According to v. 14 she recognized Peter's voice, which indicates that she knew him well. She may have heard him teaching. Thus the slave woman Rhoda was not someone separate from the group of those who were gathered together."[2] What we know of the participation of slaves in the early church makes this a very plausible theory. Although I must confess that we have no explicit statement as evidence, this was likely a house church over which she presided, based on what we know of other house churches.[3] Because Peter immediately goes to this house after being released from prison, the likelihood is that a house church had been meeting there for some

---

1. For example, Grenz with Muirkjesbo, *Women in the Church*, 81.

2. Reimer, *Women in the Acts of the Apostles: A Feminist Liberation Perspective* (in German), 242. Cf. Schottroff, *Lydia's Impatient Sisters*, 125–26. F. Scott Spencer, on the other hand, assumes that Rhoda was Mary's slave (*Dancing Girls*, 153).

3. For an excellent discussion of the origin and nature of the house churches, see Fiorenza, *In Memory of Her*, 175–84.

time.[4] Reimer argues further "[I]t is clear from the text that a community gathered in Jerusalem at Mary's house, and we may certainly conclude from this that Mary was engaged in the daily work of organization and preaching."[5] Although Reimer may have stated her point more forcefully than the evidence supports, what she says is certainly a plausible deduction from the meager evidence we have.

Stanton refers to this Mary as the sister of Barnabus but offers no evidence for this conclusion.[6] (Col 4:10 *could* be read as supporting this theory.) This fact is not particularly relevant to the present study, so I will leave it aside. What I want to emphasize is that, once more, we find a woman who is neither defined by a husband nor submissive to any male, as far as our information goes. She is identified by her son, John Mark, but there is no indication that she was in any way subject to him. She possessed a house sufficiently large for a sizable number of Christians to congregate and most likely presided over a church that met in her house.

---

4. Cf. Grenz with Muirkjesbo, *Women in the Church*, 81.

5. Reimer, *Women in the Acts of the Apostles: A Feminist Liberation Perspective* (in German), 242.

6. Stanton, *The Woman's Bible*, II:146.

32

Joanna

MENTION OF JOANNA IN the Gospels is limited to Luke 8:3 and 24:10. In the former passage she is referred to as the wife of Chuza, Herod's steward. She is listed among the names of women who were not only following Jesus during his ministry, but who were supporting (*diēkonoun*) him and his disciples out of their private means.¹ In the latter passage she is among the women who came to Jesus's tomb to anoint his body with spices. What can be said of this woman based upon such scant evidence? Perhaps Bauckham's summary is as good as any, although at some points he may be claiming more than the evidence supports:

> Joanna was born into one of the prominent and wealthy Jewish families of Galilee and grew up in one of the small castles that dotted the Galilean hills. Her parents arranged her marriage for her at an early age, and like most Jewish girls, she was married when she reached puberty. The marriage was made for political advantage, to promote her family's alliance with Herod Antipas's rule in Galilee. Her husband was the Nabatean nobleman Chuza, who had recently come to Herod's court in the entourage of the young Nabatean princess who became Herod's wife. Herod had soon promoted him to finance minister of his realm. To marry Joanna he adopted Jewish religion, though this was to his advantage in any case if he was to make his career in Herod's administration.²

Joanna obviously was held in high esteem in the Orthodox Christian tradition, as indicated by the painting of her by the iconographer and

---

1. Schottroff has argued that *ek tōn hyparchontōn autais* conveys a much broader idea than merely supporting with their possessions. She suggests the translation "according to what was possible for them in their circumstances." See Schottroff, *Lydia's Impatient Sisters*, 210–11; 272 n. 122.

2. Bauckham, *Gospel Women*, 195.

priest, Luke Dingman.³ Moltmann-Wendel has published another art work by Adrian Collaert depicting her as a saint and as *uxor Chuza procuratoris Herodis* ("wife of Chuza, administrator of Herod").⁴ This would seem to argue against Witherington's suggestion (below) that she divorced Chuza and married Andronicus. Joanna was probably honored as both a saint and an apostle. That she was an apostle in at least a general sense may be deduced from the text of Luke itself. Joanna and the group who came to Jesus's tomb reported the resurrection to the eleven *and to the rest* (emphasis mine) (Luke 24:9). This action leads to the question of whether she was an apostle in any "official" sense. Although the answer to this is often negative, it's probably been based more on the presupposition that a woman could not be an apostle than on any real evidence.

Bauckham, followed most recently by Ben Witherington, III, has advanced the idea that the Joanna of Luke is the same person as the Junia of Romans 16:7.⁵ Their basic argument is that Junia is the Latin equivalent of the Hebrew name Joanna. They also point out that particularly those who moved about in the more elite circles of Roman society often chose Roman names as a matter of convenience. This obviously requires an explanation of the association of Andronicus with Junia in Romans 16:7. At this point, Bauckham and Witherington go in different directions with their explanation of this association. Bauckham suggests that Chuza simply chose the Greek name Andronicus, which would have been more familiar to Roman Jews than his Nabatean name, and so we are still dealing with the man mentioned as Joanna's husband in Luke.⁶ Witherington takes a different, and more speculative, approach. He assumes Joanna could not have had any personal wealth of her own, and that her hus-

---

3. Witherington, "Joanna—Apostle of the Lord or Jailbait," 12.

4. Moltmann-Wendel, *The Women Around Jesus* (in German), 130.

5. Bauckham, *Gospel Women*, 109–202; Ben Witherington III, "Joanna: Apostle of the Lord—or Jailbait?" 12–14, 46. Elisabeth Moltmann-Wendel, writing more than two decades before either Bauckham or Witherington, explores some other possibilities concerning the relationship of Joanna with her husband. One is that Chuza was no longer alive when Joanna was following Jesus. Another is that they had mutually agreed to her following Jesus. Still another possibility is that we simply have an example of one leaving *everything*, husband included, to follow Jesus. She seems more inclined to the latter view, in that it would possibly explain why Joanna has never received much "press," that is, such a woman would set a dangerous example in a patriarchal society. See Moltmann-Wendel, *The Women around Jesus* (in German), 134–38.

6. Bauckham, *Gospel Women*, 198.

band resented her contributing to the ministry of a little-known, radical prophet like Jesus. (This would seem to go against the text of Luke 8:3, which refers to the women [*haitines*] as contributing to Jesus's ministry out of their private means (*tōn hyparxhontōn*). He further speculates that Chuza divorced her because of this, and she then married the Christian Andronicus.[7] Although plausible enough, nothing in the text supports the idea of any divorce or re-marriage. Joanna is simply referred to as the wife of Chuza, Herod's steward. Both Bauckham and Witherington argue that regardless of whether Junia is to be identified with Luke's Joanna or not (see further discussion below), she was a highly esteemed member of the apostolic circle, and not just a person who was held in high esteem by those who were apostles.

Morris has posed an interesting question: Were Joanna and the other women on the list members of a group of female apostles paralleling the Twelve? She writes, "Did this group of women constitute a parallel to the Twelve? There is a mosaic in the *Titulus* Church of Saint Praxedis that suggests it. There is a double circle around the doorway of the chapel of Saint Zeno consisting of the busts of the apostles with Jesus in the center and of the busts of eight women together with Our Lady [*sic*] in the center and two deacons on either side of her. It certainly gives the impression of a tradition of a collateral group of apostles, of men and women."[8]

We are justified in suspecting that there was a great deal more to this woman Joanna than surviving records tell us. She clearly defied the conventions and mores of her society and chose an independent course of life as a follower of Jesus. Regardless of whether her husband was alive or dead at this time, this was a very courageous and unusual thing for a woman to do. As Parales puts it, "Perhaps the reason Joanna left her whimsical court life was because Jesus healed her, either of evil spirits or of sickness. She had discovered something her court life and marriage to an important political figure could not give her, and she was assertive enough to leave it behind for a more meaningful life. Joanna hardly behaved like an obedient or submissive wife, and Jesus never rebuked her for her actions and courage."[9]

---

7. Witherington, "Joanna: Apostle of the Lord—or Jailbait?" 14, 46.
8. Joan Morris, *The Lady Was a Bishop*, 114.
9. Parales, *Hidden Voices*, 39.

33

Prisca/Priscilla

THE STORY OF PRISCA is embedded at various points in the accounts of the ministry of Paul in the Christian Testament. We have more information about Prisca and her husband Aquila in the New Testament than of any other pair of missionary partners.[1] Three times she is referred to as Prisca, and three times by the diminutive form Priscilla (see Acts 18:2, 18, 26; Rom 16:3; 1 Cor 16:19; 2 Tim 4:19). We first encounter her in Corinth (Acts 18:2) as having recently arrived from Rome in the wake of the expulsion of Jews by the emperor Claudius. This took place somewhere around the year 49 CE.[2] Apparently Prisca and her husband Aquila were tentmakers (though some think the more general term "leather workers" is the better translation) and this seems to have brought them together with Paul, who was of the same trade. (The major problem with the interpretation is that the word translated "tentmaker" is used nowhere else in the Christian Testament and only sparingly in secular Greek literature.[3])

When Paul left Corinth for Ephesus, Prisca and Aquila came with him to Ephesus. When Paul left Ephesus, he left Prisca and Aquila behind (in charge of the church there?). Be that as it may, Prisca and Aquila took aside an Alexandrian Jew named Apollos, who was a powerful speaker but who knew nothing about Christianity beyond the baptism of John (Acts 18:25), and "explained to him the way of God more accurately" (Acts 18:26). And less we miss the obvious, Prisca teaches in the very city where Paul (or a later Paulinist?) said women should not teach.[4] Levine comments, "The account of Priscilla, who is credited in Acts 18:26 (together

---

1. Kraemer & D'Angelo, eds., *Women and Christian Origins*, 202.
2. Reimer, *Women in the Acts of the Apostles*, 213.
3. See, for example, ibid., 199–201.
4. Cf. Gritz, *Paul, Women Teachers, and the Mother Goddess*, 81.

with her husband, Aquila) with the proper instruction of the sophisticated Alexandrian Apollos, suggests that Priscilla herself was sufficiently educated to have some credibility with one schooled in allegorical exegesis."[5] As I note below, some of the "church fathers" attempted to deny the fact that Prisca was a teacher equal to, if not superior to, her husband, while others have freely admitted her status as both teacher and preacher. Tertullian (second century CE) said clearly "by the holy Prisca the gospel is preached." John Chrysostom (fourth century CE) goes even further. He calls her "a teacher of teachers."[6] Others could be cited as well.

As early as Clement of Alexandria (?–c. 215 CE[7]) some were already attempting to deny that Prisca and Aquila were a normal married couple engaged in missionary activity. This effort often took the form of claiming that Prisca and Aquila had a "spiritual marriage" in which no sexual relations were involved. This was often coupled with the idea that the woman in this sort of partnership only ministered to other women.[8] Although belief in such spiritual marriages does appear in Christian history, it is by no means certain that such a belief was held as early as the late first century CE when the book of Acts was written. Upon closer examination this belief is shown to be just another chauvinistic attempt to deny the obvious—namely, that women did participate in Christian missionary work on an equal basis with men during the early development of the church. Only with the development of an all-male priesthood and the increasing control of the church by that priesthood were women systematically excluded from official places of leadership in the church.[9] Much more needs to be said on this subject, but to pursue it here would take me too far afield from the parameters of this study.[10]

Other attempts to dilute what the text says about Prisca are reflected in the Greek text itself. In Acts 18:2, some manuscripts have Paul staying only with him (i.e., Aquila). Others leave off the word "together" in

---

5. Levine, *Women Like This*, 231. See also Getty-Sullivan, *Women in the New Testament*, 156.

6. Cited in Parales, *Hidden Voices*, 68.

7. Walker, *A History of the Christian Church*, 72.

8. Kraemer and D'Angelo, *Women and Christian Origins*, 203.

9. Cf. Reimer, *Women in the Acts of the Apostles*, 217.

10. For those interested in pursuing such matters, a good starting point would be Ranft, *Women and Spiritual Equality in Christian Tradition* and Eisen, *Women Officeholders in Early Christianity*.

the statement that Paul worked together with Aquila and Prisca. In Acts 18:26, some reverse the names so that Aquila appears before Priscilla.[11] Once again, we see evidence of attempts to subordinate Prisca to Aquila and place her in her "proper place." The lateness of the manuscripts in which these changes occur is a dead giveaway that they are not original.

One of the more striking aspects in the account of Prisca and Aquila in Acts is the fact that, in defiance of all first-century conventions, Prisca is named before her husband Aquila. (This would be somewhat like addressing Mrs. and Mr. John Doe in a modern setting.) Not only here, but in four of the six times this couple is mentioned in the New Testament, her name appears first. No doubt with tongue in cheek, Bushnell comments, "He (Paul) actually dares to put this woman's 'head' on behind! How that would scandalize the proprieties of modern theology!"[12] Mauldin suggests the placement of Prisca's name before Aquila indicates that "probably . . . she was more important for the Christian community—whether by virtue of nobility, personality, or spirituality is unclear."[13] In a similar vein Dunn writes, "The most obvious deduction is that Prisca was the more dominant of the two or of higher social status, and she may either have provided the financial resources for the business or have been the brains behind it."[14] Kapp refers to a number of conjectures based upon the order of the names and concludes, "The best explanation seems to be that she was the stronger character."[15] "Whatever we conjecture as to why the biblical authors wrote in this fashion, we say too little if we pass over this unusual way of referring to a married couple by saying that 'Luke may simply have wanted to give greater honor to the woman.' Such a comment overlooks the significance of the biblical authors' obvious departure from the norms of their day."[16] Regarding the fact that Prisca is mentioned first in the context of the instruction of Apollos, Byrne comments this possibly indicates

---

11. For a more detailed discussion, see Reimer, *Women in the Acts of the Apostles*, 197–99.

12. Bushnell, *God's Word to Women*, 192.

13. *Mercer Dictionary of the Bible*, s.v. "Priscilla and Aquila."

14. Hubbard & Barker, gen. eds., *Romans 9–16*, 892. For the suggestion that nobility of birth placed Prisca first see Barclay, *The Gospel of Luke*, 230–31; Keener, *Paul, Women and Wives*, 241. See also Groothuis, *Good News for Women*, 194 (but note the inaccuracies in the number of times the name Priscilla/Prisca appears and also the omission of Acts 18:2 & 1 Cor 16:19 from references thereunto [see above]).

15. *International Standard Bible Encyclopaedia*, s.v. "Aquila."

16. Grenz with Muirkjesbo, *Women in the Church*, 82.

that she took the major part in the instruction.[17] Kraemer and D'Angelo take the matter a step further: "Taken together, the facts that Prisca may have been perceived as having a higher social status than Aquila and that much of her leadership would have been exercised in a household setting means that there is good reason to believe that her influence in Pauline Christianity extended even beyond that of her partner."[18]

Prisca's being placed in the role of teaching (*ektithēmi*), even along with her husband, could scarcely be considered accidental or as due to scribal error. Placing a woman in the role of teacher in the first century CE would have jolted anyone who read this. The verb *ektithēmi* (translated "explained" in Acts 18:26) literally means "to cast out," or "to expose." It is used in the latter sense in Acts 7:21. In the only two other passages where this verb occurs in the Christian Testament (outside the present passage where the subject is Priscilla and Aquila) it refers to an open and public proclamation of the Gospel by Peter (Acts 11:4) and Paul (Acts 28:23). All this adds up to a rather strong argument that Prisca was a Christian teacher and leader on a par with, if not superior to, her husband. That Paul himself accorded her this status is demonstrated by his reference to Prisca and Aquila as fellow workers in Christ (Rom 16:3). "This expression, not so very frequently employed by Paul, signifies much. By its use Priscilla and Aquila are legitimized official Evangelists and Teachers [sic]."[19] To be more specific, the word *synergoi* ("fellow workers"; KJV, "helpers"[20]) is used in the Pauline writings twelve times and only once in the rest of the Christian Testament. The list of those whom Paul designated as fellow workers includes, in addition to Prisca and Aquila, one Urbanus (Rom. 16:9), Apollos (1 Cor 3:9), the congregation at Corinth (which certainly included a number of unnamed women as well as men) (2 Cor 1:24), Titus (2 Cor 8:23), Epaphroditus (Phil 2:25), Euodia, Syntyche, Clement, plus others "whose names are in the book of life" (Phil 4:2–3), Aristarchus, Mark, Jesus Justus (Col 4:10–11), Timothy (1 Thess 3:2), Philemon (Phlm 1), Aristarchus, Demas, and Luke (Phlm 24). That Prisca is accorded any

---

17. Byrne, *Paul and the Christian Woman*, 71.
18. Kraemer & D'Angelo, *Women and Christian Origins*, 204, 241.
19. Bushnell, *God's Word to Women*, 196.
20. Even so conservative a scholar as Ryrie concedes, "It would be difficult to prove that the 'helping' did not include public teaching and even possibly missionary work." See Boldrey and Boldrey, *Chauvinist or Feminist*, 20 n. 7.

place whatever in this distinguished company is remarkable—that she is placed in a dominant role borders on the miraculous.

As Reimer has well said, "Priscilla is owed 'reparation' in the sense 'that she is to be recalled again and again to memory in the fullness of her womanhood: as wife, tentmaker, highly valued co-worker of Paul and acquaintance of Apollos.'"[21] She further offers these words as an appropriate conclusion to the discussion of Prisca: "[N]ot only in Paul's writing, but also in Luke's, Priscilla can be recognized as a highly esteemed missionary who is understood as Paul's 'co-worker' and who stands as an equal not only alongside Aquila, but also in the company of Paul and other missionaries. Not least we should emphasize that, in Acts, Priscilla is the only married woman for whom marriage poses no obstacle to the totality of her work on behalf of justice."[22] As Ruether has aptly stated, "The right to preach was given to women by the Holy Spirit at Pentecost, and women in the apostolic age, such as Anna and the daughters of Philip and Priscilla, taught in public. It is male tyranny against the explicit word of Scripture that has denied women the right to preach and has kept women from the education by which their superior gifts might be evident."[23]

---

21. Reimer, *Women in the Acts of the Apostles*, 217.
22. Ibid., 219.
23. Ruether, *Women and Redemption*, 120.

34

Phoebe

THE MENTION OF PHOEBE in Romans 16:1–2 is among the strongest evidence that women were in positions of leadership in the early church. In this passage Paul commended Phoebe as a *diakonos* of the church at Cenchrae. The word *diakonos* is the direct source of the English word "deacon." In the Greek language no difference between the masculine and feminine form of this word exists, so, in theory at least, it could refer to either a man or a woman. The original meaning of the word is somewhat obscure but seems to have been "one who waits on tables," a rather lowly form of service in the ancient world.[1] From its original usage the word came to be used in the general sense of servant and eventually of an "office" in the church. In the Christian Testament it is found in the general sense of servant eight times (Matt 20:26, 22:13, 23:11; Mark 9:35, 10:43; John 2:5, 9; 12:26). It is used twenty-two times in the more specialized sense of a function in the church.[2] Of these twenty-two usages, the KJV translates *diakonos* as "minister" eighteen times, as "deacon" three times—and only in Romans 16:1 as "servant!"[3] Roberts aptly points out that "The churches of that day had no *servants*, in the ordinary sense of the word servant. The churches were poor. Their meetings were held in private houses. They had no church edifices."[4] Furthermore, the word is unambiguously applied to a female only in the latter passage. What explanation could there be for translating this word twenty-one times of its specialized usage as either "minister" or "deacon," and this once only as "servant"—except for the *assumption* that because Phoebe was a woman

---

1. *Theological Dictionary of the New Testament*, s. v. *"diaconos."*
2. Rom 13:4 (twice), 15:8, 16:1; 1 Cor 3:5; 2 Cor 3:6, 6:4; 11:15 (twice), 23; Gal 2:17; Eph 3:7, 6:21; Phil 1:1; Col 1:7, 23, 25; 4:7; 1 Thess 3:2; 1 Tim 3:8, 12; 4:6.
3. Cf. Scanzoni and Hardesty, *All We're Meant to Be*, 67.
4. Roberts, *Ordaining Women*, 64 (page citations are to the reprint edition).

she could not be in a leadership position in a church? As Wiley notes in her recent work, "There is no indication of any difference when the title *diakonos* is given to Phoebe and when it is given to Timothy."[5] Yet only with the recently published NRSV Bible and the TNT was the word translated "deacon" in Phoebe's case. The NEB translates it with the phrase "who holds office." The REB renders it as "minister." (Perhaps we should note here that the church "offices" were not clearly developed at this point in Christian history. Both "minister" and "deacon" were rather fluid ideas and perhaps were not in every case differentiated at all.) Versions as different from one another as the KJV, ASV, NASB, and NIV all translate *diakonos* as "servant" in Romans 16:1. Beck uses the synonym "worker." The TEV and LNT paraphrase with "who serves" and "She has worked hard" respectively. Williams, the RSV, Phillips, and Amplified New Testament translate it "deaconess," which does not have the same ring to it as the word "deacon." Furthermore, the word "deaconess" is anachronistic, in that no usage of this term in Christian literature has ever come to light until well into the second century CE.[6] Nunnally-Cox puts the matter bluntly, saying, "There is no term 'deaconess' here or anywhere else in the New Testament."[7] As Spencer has pointed out, the reference to Phoebe as *diakonos of a particular church* is all the more reason to translate the word as "minister" rather than "servant."[8] Even this translation, however, may be misleading, as Getty-Sullivan has noted: "The New American Bible avoids using 'deacon' for Phoebe and uses instead 'minister,' a more generic term that can more easily suggest a subordinate function considered proper for a woman. These sleights of pen (what a pun!) illustrate that a translation is an interpretation and that an androcentric bias has been at work in the reading of the biblical texts for a long time."[9] Further, as Groothuis has pointed out, "The term used to describe Phoebe's ministry is also used by Paul to describe the ministries of Apollos, Timothy, Tychicus, Epaphras, and, most frequently, Paul himself."[10] Dietrick has well summarized the

---

5. Wiley, *Paul and the Galatian Women*, 93.

6. Cf. Jensen, *God's Self-Confident Daughters*, 60. Some have even argued that there was no such "office" as deaconess until the late fourth century CE in the Eastern Church. See, e.g., Swidler, *Biblical Affirmations of Woman*, 311.

7. Nunnally-Cox, *Foremothers*, 133.

8. Aida Besancon Spencer, *Beyond the Curse*, 115.

9. Getty-Sullivan, *Women in the New Testament*, 256.

10. Groothuis, *Good News for Women*, 196; See also Byrne, *Paul and the Christian Woman*, 69–70.

significance of one of Phoebe's titles: "Paul not only virtually pronounces Priscilla a fellow-Apostle [sic] and fellow-bishop (Romans, chap. 16, verses 3–5) [sic], but specially commends Phebe [sic], a Greek woman, as a minister (diakonos), which, as we have seen, may be legitimately interpreted either presbyter, bishop, or Apostle."[11]

An even stronger indication of Phoebe's function as a leader surfaces in Romans 16:2. There she is referred to as a *prostatis* of many, and of Paul himself. Again, the translations of this word are most interesting. The NASB. RSV, ASV, and Amplified New Testament translate it as "helper." The KJV renders it with the synonym "succourer." The LNT paraphrases it "has helped many." The NIV, TNT, NEB, REB, and TEV paraphrase it "has been a great help." Clearly the idea of "helper" has dominated the translations of *prostatis* in this passage. The NRSV, however, translates it as "benefactor," as does the TNIV. Beck translates it as "protector," and Williams has maintained the same idea by the paraphrase, "has given protection." (These last two translations are most interesting, in view of the fact that Phoebe is explicitly said to have been a *prostatis* of *Paul*, as well as others!) I would again raise the question as to the degree to which Phoebe's gender has influenced most of these translations.

The major difficulty (other than false assumptions) we encounter in translating *prostatis* is that it appears nowhere else in the Christian Testament. As Swidler affirms, "Paul also refers to Phoebe as a 'ruler' (prostatis), not as a "helper," as it is usually, and unwarrantedly, translated; the word ... always means ruler, leader, or protector in all Greek literature."[12] Gritz states bluntly, "For Phoebe, *prostatis* meant helper, patroness and leader."[13] Bilezikian adds the idea of a legal official who spoke on behalf of aliens to the list, then comments, "Phoebe had apparently been able to use her good offices to protect or deliver a number of Christian leaders in critical circumstances, including Paul himself."[14]

Because we do not have the luxury of comparing ways in which the word *prostatis* is used in other contexts in the Christian Testament, I will examine what evidence we find in the Jewish Scriptures that may shed light on this term. We have five occurrences of a slightly variant form

---

11. Stanton, *The Woman's Bible*, II, 154.
12. Swidler, *Biblical Affirmations of Woman*, 310.
13. Gritz, *Paul, Women Teachers, and the Mother Goddess*, 81.
14. Bilezikian, *Beyond Sex Roles*, 205.

prostatēs in the Greek version of the Jewish Scriptures. Once it is used of the overseers of King David's property (1 Chr 27:31). Once it is used of the overseers of the king's works (1 Chr 27:31). Once it is used of Solomon's chief officers (2 Chr 8:10). Once it is used of King Joash's chief officers (2 Chr 24:11). Its final usage designates the officers of the chief priest (2 Chr 24:11). Quite obviously these who were designated by the term *prostatēs* in the Jewish Scriptures were no ordinary helpers, but were in every case highly authoritative people. Thus the translations of the NRSV that Beck and Williams cited above are made much more plausible than any of the others.

I will now take one other approach to evidence in the Christian Testament that should be considered in any attempt to translate *prostatis*. Because we do not have the noun form *prostatis* anywhere else, let us look at the verb form *proistēmi* on which it is built. The basic meaning of this verb is "to stand before," "to preside," "to rule," "to govern."[15] Let us examine this verb's usage in the Christian Testament and see what light it may shed on the meaning of *prostatis* as applied to Phoebe.

We have a total of eight occurrences of the verb in the Christian Testament, with six of them found in the Pastoral Epistles. In Romans 12:8 a participle of the verb appears, which is variously translated "leads" (NASB, NEB), "ruleth" (KJV), "gives aid" (RSV), and "wields authority" (Phillips). In 2 Thessalonians 5:12 the same participle is rendered "have charge over" (NASB), "are over" (KJV, RSV), and "leaders" (Phillips, NEB). In 1 Timothy 3:4, again the participial form, it is translated "manages" (RSV, NASB, NEB), "ruleth" (KJV), and "have proper authority" (Phillips). In the next verse the infinitive of the verb is variously translated "to manage" (NASB, RSV, NEB), "ruleth" (KJV), and "control" (Phillips). In 1 Timothy 3:12 the participle appears again and is translated "managers" (NASB), "managing" (RSV, NEB), "ruling" (KJV), and "control" (Phillips). The participle appears once more in 1 Timothy 5:17 and is rendered "rule" (NASB, KJV, RSV), "with a gift of leadership" (Phillips), and "who do well as leaders" (NEB). The final two occurrences are found in Titus 3:8, 14; both of which are present infinitives. The object of the infinitive in these two passages is "good deeds." In the other six occurrences the object is a person or persons. The translations given above show unmistakably

---

15. Abbott-Smith, *Manual Greek Lexicon of the New Testament*, 3rd ed., s.v. "*proistēmi*." Cf. Scanzoni & Hardesty, *All We're Meant to Be*, 87; Swidler, *Biblical Affirmations of Woman*, 310–11: Gritz, *Paul, Women Teachers, and the Mother Goddess*, 81.

that where people are the object this verb indicates authority and control over those people. This being the case, the likelihood that the noun form *prostatis* also implies authority is considerable. As Parales has noted, "Within the New Testament, the verb form of *prostatis* referred to leading, having charge over others, the ruling activities of elders, and managing households."[16] In the words of Spencer, "The most likely significance of *prostatis* is its common meaning of a leader and ruler." She also points out that "in the later church the term was used of civil rulers, ecclesiastical rulers and bishops."[17] Groothuis expresses a similar opinion: "Paul also describes Phoebe as a benefactor or patron (*prostatis*) of the church, which implies a position of prominence and authority."[18]

Secular usage of *prostatis* supports the opinions mentioned above. In secular Greek this word is applied to kings, governors, military leaders—just about every type of leader that existed in the ancient world.[19] We are long overdue for giving Phoebe the stature she deserves. She was in authority as a deacon/minister of the church at Cenchrae. I would endorse Spencer's conclusion that "only an English translator's bias will term Phoebe a 'servant' and 'helper' rather than a 'minister' and 'leader.'"[20] As Fiorenza has pointed out, one of the more significant things about Phoebe is what is not said about her. She is not described as either a virgin or a widow. Nor is she in any way associated with a husband. There is no evidence she was married. "The one role mentioned is an ecclesial one."[21] As MacDonald comments, "Scholars have generally viewed Phoebe as a wealthy, independent woman, who may even have moved in more elite circles than Paul."[22] In the words of Elizabeth A. Castelli, "If one further notes that Phoebe is not named in relation to her father, husband, brother, or guardian—a striking silence in the text's description of her—one might well assume that Phoebe lived and acted independently from the more typical legal relations that situated women primarily in terms of their

---

16. Parales, *Hidden Voices*, 64. See also Swidler, *Biblical Affirmations of Woman*, 310–11.

17. Aida Besancon Spencer, *Beyond the Curse*, 116–17.

18. Rebecca Groothuis, *Good News for Women*, 196.

19. See *Theological Dictionary of the New Testament*, s.v. "*proistēmi*."

20. Cited in Hull, *Equal to Serve*, 118.

21. Cited in Murphy, *The Word according to Eve*, 178.

22. Kraemer and D'Angelo, *Women and Christian Origins*, 209. See also Grenz with Muirkjesbo, *Women in the Church*, 89.

relationship to male family members. Indeed, that Phoebe is characterized only once in a familial idiom—'our sister'—suggests that her social identity is fully integrated into her new Christian family."[23]

---

23. Cited in Wiley, *Paul and the Gentile Women*, 93–94.

35

Junia/Julia

Before discussing this woman, let me explain why I have two names listed for her. In Romans 16:7, the name in English translations is consistently Junia or Junias. (If there are exceptions, I am unaware of them.) The reason for my including the name Julia is very simple—the oldest Greek manuscript of Romans known today, Papyrus Manuscript 46, reads "Julia" instead of "Junia."[1]

Romans 16 presents a woman who was not only a deacon/minister of the church at Cenchrae, but also a woman who was an apostle. In Romans 16:7 Paul wrote, "Greet Andronicus and Junia, my kinsmen, and my fellow prisoners, who are outstanding among the apostles, who also were in Christ before me."

As Groothuis notes, "In recent centuries translators and commentators have earnestly endeavored to explain that Junia was either not a woman or, if a woman, not an apostle but merely esteemed by the apostles."[2] Therefore, to support my claim that Junia was a female apostle, two things must be established: (1) that Junia was a woman, and (2) that she was in fact an apostle, not merely held in high esteem by those who were apostles. As to the former, Spencer cites Origen, John Chrysostom, and Jerome as assuming that Junia was a woman.[3] More significantly, the fact that the earliest manuscript of Romans (plus a few lesser manuscripts) reads "Julia" instead of "Junia" could, on its own, demonstrate that the status of apostle could be held by a woman, if we can demonstrate that Andronicus and Junias were in fact apostles. I will return to this point later.

---

1. Nestle and Aland, *Novum Testamentum Graece*, 439. For dating and description of this manuscript, see Kenyon, *Our Bible and the Ancient Manuscripts*, 188–89.

2. Rebecca Groothuis, *Good News for Women*, 194–95.

3. Aida Besancon Spencer, *Beyond the Curse*, 101. See also Groothuis, *Good News for Women*, 195.

As Dunn,[4] Spencer,[5] and others have noted, Junias has been widely assumed to be a contraction of the masculine name Julianus. The same two authors point out that the masculine form Junias has been found nowhere in extant literature. In sharp contrast, P. Lampe has pointed out no less than two-hundred-fifty examples of the feminine name Junia.[6] Spencer notes that Moulton and Howard cite Junia as a Latin woman's name in their *A Grammar of New Testament Greek*.[7] Commentators consistently assumed that Junias was a woman up to the latter part of the thirteenth century CE, when Aegidus of Rome referred to Andronicus and Junias as two men.[8] Swidler affirms the same point and comments, "It is odd that it is only in more modern times that Christian writers have strained to make Junia into a male name; misogynism apparently still persists."[9]

We need to look at one other grammatical point regarding this name. In the Greek text the accusative case form *Iounian* is found. The spelling, except for the accent, would therefore be the same whether the name were masculine or feminine. Because all of the earliest manuscripts of the New Testament were written without accents, the speculation that the name is masculine was made much easier.

I think I have sufficiently established the fact that Junia in Romans 16:7 is in fact a woman. The next task is to establish that she was an apostle. In order to avoid the specter of a female apostle, some interpreters have taken the phrase "outstanding among the apostles" to mean only that these two people were held in high esteem by those who were apostles. Keener raises a serious doubt concerning such an interpretation, saying, "Since they were imprisoned with him, Paul knows them well enough to recommend them without appealing to the other apostles, *whose judgment he never cites on such matters* (emphasis mine), and the Greek is most naturally read as claiming that they were apostles."[10] Spencer makes

---

4. Hubbard and Barker, gen. eds., *Romans 9–16*, 894.

5. Aida Besancon Spencer, *Beyond the Curse*, 101.

6. Cited in Hubbard & Barker, gen. eds., *Romans 9–16*, 894. Cf. Kraemer & D'Angelo, *Women and Christian Origins*, 109–10; Parales, *Hidden Voices*, 66.

7. Aida Besancon Spencer, *Beyond the Curse*, 102 n. 5. Cf. Keener, *Paul, Women and Wives*, 241–42.

8. Cf. ibid., 101; Rebecca Groothuis, *Good News for Women*, 195; Murphy, *The Word according to Eve*, 179; Eisen, *Women Officeholders in Early Christianity*, 47.

9. Swidler, *Biblical Affirmations of Woman*, 299.

10. Keener, *Paul, Women and Wives*, 242. See also Bilezikian, *Beyond Sex Roles*, 301 n. 54; Grenz with Muirkjesbo, *Women in the Church*, 93–95.

Junia/Julia

the grammatical point more explicit, pointing out that "the preposition *en* always has the idea of 'within.'" She then goes on to say, "The meaning 'by' would be rendered by prepositions signifying 'with' such as *para* or *pros* (Luke 2:52; Acts 2:47)."[11] S. F. Hunter, though arguing for the masculine name Junias, agrees that the interpretation of these two as apostles is "probably correct."[12] Keener gives an excellent summary of the matter. "Those who favor the view that Junia was not a female apostle do so because of their prior assumption that women could not be apostles, not because of any evidence in the text."[13] Or, as Kroeger comments, "One can only acknowledge that learned gentlemen have inserted into the rendering of this passage their own preconceived notions."[14] In Parales's words, "The woman Junia was not only one among the apostles, but she also was considered an outstanding apostle."[15] "With the rediscovery of the New Testament apostle Junia the centuries-old opinion (still emphatically maintained by the Roman Catholic Church) that in the apostolic period there were only male apostles has been finally disproved."[16]

---

11. Aida Besancon Spencer, *Beyond the Curse*, 102. Cf. Parales, *Hidden Voices*, 66.
12. *International Standard Bible Encyclopaedia*, s.v. "Junias."
13. Keener, *Paul, Women and Wives*, 242.
14. Cited in Knowles, *Let Her Be*, 160.
15. Parales, *Hidden Voices*, 66.
16. Eisen, *Women Officeholders in Early Christianity*, 48. See also Gritz, *Paul, Women Teachers, and the Mother Goddess*, 82; Preato, "A Female Apostle: Was Junia a Man or a Woman?" 23–25; and especially Pederson, *The Lost Apostle*.

36

Euodia and Syntyche

THE SOLE MENTION OF Euodia and Syntyche occurs in Philippians 4:2–3. From the meager information given, we can discern that Paul considered them as laborers with him in the Gospel, and as included with those "whose names were in the book of life." The verb for laborer that Paul uses here means to strive as an athlete.[1] "Clearly, if Paul used such a strong verb, these women did not simply supply material support for Paul and the other men but preached, taught, and spread the gospel as vigorously as they."[2]

In view of Paul's encouragement to them to live in harmony in the Lord, we may safely infer that Euodia and Syntyche had some sort of disagreement between them that in some way affected the church. Paul encourages a man identified only as "true comrade" (*gnēsie syzyge*) to assist these women in working out their differences. It is possible that *syzyge* is actually a proper noun instead of the description "comrade" or "yokefellow" (KJV). Because the earliest Greek manuscripts were written in all block capital letters it is sometimes impossible to know whether or not a word is a proper noun.

Some have suggested that Euodia and Syntyche's conflict was with Paul instead of (or as well as) with each other.[3] Probably they were in some sort of leadership position in the church so that their disagreement affected the harmony of the entire church at Philippi. One suggestion has been that they were leaders of two separate house churches at Philippi and had come to see each other as competitors instead of co-workers.[4] "Paul

---

1. Cf. Grenz with Muirkjesbo, *Women in the Church*, 84–85.
2. Swidler, *Biblical Affirmations of Woman*, 295. Cf. Parales, *Hidden Voices*, 68–69.
3. Cf. Kraemer & D'Angelo, *Women and Christian Origins*, 204.
4. Cf. Byrne, *Paul and the Christian Woman*, 69; Knowles, *Let Her Be*, 164.

considers the authority of both women in the community at Philippi so great that he fears that their dissension could do serious damage to the Christian mission.... At stake here, then, are not personal disagreements or quarrels but the shared ground and the purpose of their equal partnership in the 'race' for the gospel."[5] In the known letters of Paul, this is the only occasion when he addresses two people by name and calls on them to iron out their difficulties.

Kraemer and D'Angelo have concluded that "With Euodia and Syntyche, we encounter indisputable evidence of women acting as leaders without male counterparts."[6] Perhaps "indisputable" is too strong a term, but I believe they are essentially correct. Keener[7] has provided an appropriate concluding comment regarding these two women. "Paul mentions only incidentally that they were women who labored with him in the gospel; we may wonder how many other women ministers remain unnamed in his writings simply because their ministry was not normally at issue with him."

---

5. Fiorenza, *In Memory of Her*, 170.
6. Kraemer & D'Angelo, *Women and Christian Origins*, 205.
7. Keener, *Paul, Women and Wives*, 242–43.

37

Lydia

As we have already seen with several other female figures in the Bible, we only get a couple of brief glimpses into the life of Lydia. She is mentioned in the Christian Testament in only three verses in Acts 16. In context, the Apostle Paul has gone out to a river where he has heard that some women were gathered for prayer. As Reimer notes, this is the only reference in the New Testament to a gathering of *women*.[1] This has led to much scholarly debate as to whether this place of prayer (*proseuchē*) was an official gathering or just an informal group of women. Obviously, those who deny the permissibility of women leading worship services, whether Jewish or Christian, tend to argue that this was an informal gathering. Others argue that this "place of prayer" served the purpose of a synagogue.[2]

Because this gathering took place on the Sabbath, we may safely assume that these women were either Jewish or Gentile "God-fearers"; more likely the latter. As Paul spoke to this gathering of women, Lydia responded to his message and, along with her *oikos* ("household"), was baptized. She then entreated Paul and Silas to stay in her house, "if they judged her to be faithful to God." Shortly thereafter we read that Paul and Silas were beaten and imprisoned. When they were released from prison they went to the house of Lydia, encouraged "the brethren," and then left the city. This strongly suggests that a house church had been formed there. "Lydia is probably a typical and early example of a constant pattern whereby wealthy and prominent women act as patrons and protectors of the early Christian movement."[3]

1. Reimer, *Women in the Acts of the Apostles*, 72.
2. For a thorough discussion of the issues involved, see ibid., 78–92.
3. Byrne, *Paul and the Christian Woman*, 67. See also Kraemer and D'Angelo, *Women and Christian Origins*, 240.

Lydia

What can we know of Lydia from these very brief references? First of all, she was apparently an independent woman, in that we find no mention of a husband or male relatives. As Schottroff notes, her house was inhabited by women. If any male had lived there (other than possibly a male slave) he would have been the paterfamilias.[4] She was head of a household that included children or slaves, or both. She was also a woman of some means, since her house was large enough for a group to meet in it. Reference to her as a seller of purple would suggest a successful businesswoman, in that purple was the color of royalty.[5] Fiorenza suggests that she might have been a freedwoman, because she came from the east and sold purple (luxury) goods.[6] Schottroff further suggests that, because she is identified by her place of origin (Lydia), she was not a woman of social standing.[7] Her profession was looked upon unfavorably because of the unpleasant smells associated with production of the purple dyes.[8] Because Lydia was originally from Thyatira in Asia Minor, her presence in Philippi likely suggests that her business required her to travel, whether to establish warehouses as Spencer suggests (below) or simply to sell her wares.[9]

One writer suggests that Lydia had come to Philippi in order to establish a warehouse so that her wares could be shipped out either east or west from there.[10] While this is a plausible suggestion we have no real evidence that would support it.

Reimer has argued extensively that Lydia was the leader of a worshipping community.[11] But despite having invited the apostles into her house and probably hosting a house church, we look in vain for any prophetic words from Lydia. She is completely compliant with Paul's words. She leaves it to him to judge whether she is worthy of the company of

---

4. Schottroff, *Lydia's Impatient Sisters*, 110. See also Reimer, *Women in the Acts of the Apostles*, 111.

5. For an argument that Lydia was not necessarily wealthy, see ibid., 99.

6. Fiorenza, *In Memory of Her*, 178. See also Getty-Sullivan, *Women in the New Testament*, 246.

7. Schottroff, *Lydia's Impatient Sisters*, 131–32. See also Murphy, *The Word according to Eve*, 188.

8. Parales, *Hidden Voices*, 70.

9. Cf. Kraemer and D'Angelo, *Women and Christian Origins*, 239–40.

10. Aida Besancon Spencer, *Beyond the Curse*, 112.

11. Reimer, *Women in the Acts of the Apostles*, 109–11.

the apostles. Although we may logically surmise, as Reimer does, that she later played a leadership role in the church in her house, "Luke" gives us no hint on this.[12]

---

12. Cf. F. Scott Spencer, *Dancing Girls*, 156.

38

Tryphaena and Tryphosa

THE SOLE REFERENCE TO Tryphaena and Tryphosa in the Bible is in Romans 16:12, where Paul sends them greetings as *tas kopiōsas* ("the workers") in the Lord. Obviously we have not much to go on in figuring out who these two women were, and what role they played. However, probing into Paul's usage of the verb for laboring may provide at least a plausible guess as to how Paul regarded them. In 1 Corinthians 15:10 Paul wrote: "But by the grace of God I am what I am, and His grace toward me did not prove vain; but I labored (*ekopiasa*) even more than all of them, yet not I, but the grace of God with me." Some think this indicates that they were missionary partners of Paul.[1] Kraemer and D'Angelo suggest that the verb (*kopiaō*) is used by Paul in a near-technical sense as denoting missionary activity.[2] In a similar vein Fiorenza writes, "It is significant, therefore, that Paul uses the same Greek verb, *kopian*, 'to labor' or 'to toil,' not only to characterize his own evangelizing and teaching but also that of women. In Rom 16:6, 12, he commends Mary, Tryphaena, Tryphosa, and Persis for having 'labored hard' in the Lord."[3] Dietrick goes a step further, placing them in the category of female apostles, but without offering any real evidence for her position.[4] Bushnell sees Paul as commanding subjection to such women as these. She bases this upon 1 Corinthians 16:15–16 where Paul writes, "Now I urge you, brethren... that you also be in subjection to such men and to everyone who helps in the work and labors (*panti tō synergounti kai kopiōnti*).

---

1. For example, Kraemer and D'Angelo, *Women and Christian Origins*, 207.
2. Ibid., 225.
3. Fiorenza, *In Memory of Her*, 169. See also Franzmann, *Romans*, 274.
4. Cited in Stanton, *The Woman's Bible*, II:154.

"Here then is a very clear command which at least included men, to 'be in subjection,' to women, who were certainly included in the body of *every one that helpeth with us and laboureth*.' (emphasis original)."[5] She makes the further point that "subjection" is not to be equated with "obedience," a point of no small significance for the whole idea of submission in regard to women and men.[6]

Any conclusions we may draw concerning Tryphaena and Tryphosa must be rather tentative. At the very least, Paul commends them as having "worked hard in the Lord." The verb he uses *may* indicate that they worked in the same manner as Paul himself. This opens up the *possibility* that they had the status as apostles, but little more can be said.

---

5. Bushnell, *God's Word to Women*, 297.
6. Ibid.

39

Nympha

ONCE AGAIN WE HAVE a woman to whom Paul sends greetings (if Paul is in fact the author of Colossians[1]) and nothing more. The greeting, however, is both to Nympha and the church in her house. If the text tells us little about Nympha, the textual history speaks volumes. It appears that from fairly ancient times the specter of a woman in charge of a house church was scandalous. The text, therefore, shows rather clear evidence of attempts to get rid of any reference to a woman's hosting a church in her house.

With the name Nympha we have a situation parallel to the name Junia, in that the accusative case form found in reference to both would be the same whether the name were masculine or feminine. Also like Junia, the name Nympha(s) is not found in Roman inscriptions as a man's name, but is found as a woman's name more than sixty times.[2]

The attempts to turn Nympha into a man require a change in the pronoun also. Accordingly, some manuscripts read "his" house, or "their" house.[3] The latter would make it appear that someone else, possibly a husband, was also involved. Fiorenza makes this summary statement: "The feminine reading is the more difficult reading and the masculine form can easily be understood as a correction of the female name since it was considered improbable or undesirable that a woman have such a leadership position."[4] Kraemer and D'Angelo make the point more bluntly: "It

---

1. Some scholars place Colossians, along with Ephesians, 2 Thessalonians, 1–2 Timothy, and Titus in the "disputed" category as possibly written by a later disciple of Paul, rather than the apostle himself.

2. Cf. Knowles, *Let Her Be*, 64.

3. For a concise presentation of the textual evidence, see Fiorenza, *In Memory of Her*, 51; Parales, *Hidden Voices*, 70–71.

4. Ibid.

is now widely recognized that the attempt to masculinize Nympha, which appears in several ancient versions of the text (and is reflected in some modern translations), is rooted in the scandal created by the existence of a woman leader of a house-church."[5]

Another approach to getting rid of the specter of a woman leading a house church is to argue that she was only host in a social sense, that is, cooking, providing refreshments, and so on. Grady, after noting that Chloe and Nympha had churches in their houses, comments, "We can assume that these women held pastoral positions." He then says parenthetically "Conservative scholars, of course, believe they were simply 'hosting' the churches in their homes—and perhaps preparing sandwiches and cookies for the after-church fellowship time."[6]

What conclusions can we draw from all this? First of all, Nympha was almost certainly a woman, and an independent woman who had her own house at that. Her tradition has survived, despite attempts to turn her into a man.[7] She is the only woman greeted by name in Colossians and Ephesians.[8] We know nothing of her wealth or status in society. She was in all probability the pastor of the church that met in her house, based upon what we know about such house churches. Eisen, by the way, notes that house churches meeting in the homes of women continued beyond the Christian Testament era.[9]

---

5. Kraemer & D'Angelo, *Women and Christian Origins*, 209.
6. Grady, *10 Lies the Church Tells Women*, 41.
7. Cf. Kraemer & D'Angelo, *Women and Christian Origins*, 244.
8. Ibid., 242.
9. Eisen, *Women Officeholders in Early Christianity*, 206.

40

Apphia

THE ONLY EXPLICIT MENTION of Apphia is in Paul's greeting in Philemon 1–2. She has been traditionally identified as Philemon's wife, although without any specific evidence. Archippus has likewise been assumed to be the son of Philemon and Apphia. If we can break free of these traditional assumptions, we may see an entirely different picture of Apphia. In the text Paul greets Philemon as "the beloved," Apphia as "the sister," and Archippus as "the fellow soldier." They are greeted in such a way as to suggest that all three were prominent in the community.[1] There is no indication of any biological relationship among any of the three. Further, when Paul greets the church in "your" house, the "your" is singular (*sou*).[2] The possibility is just as strong that Philemon, Apphia, and Archippus were co-leaders of the church that met in Philemon's home as that they were father, mother, and son. This is not a new suggestion by any means. Fiorenza has obviously made this assumption. "Paul greets Apphia 'our sister,' who together with Philemon and Archippus was a leader of the house church in Colossae to which the letter to Philemon was written (Phlm 2)."[3] More cautiously, Swidler has written, "Although one house church at Colossae was in the house of a woman (Nympha's), a second was not. Nevertheless even in that one a woman, Apphia, was singled out by Paul, apparently as a leader in that house church."[4] Kraemer and D'Angelo write, "Apphia was evidently a leader. She may indeed be a member of the household of Philemon where the community meets, but

---

1. Kraemer and D'Angelo, *Women and Christian Origins*, 206.

2. Belleville is in error at this point. The "you" in the greeting of v. 3 is plural, but singular following the word "house." See Belleville, *Women Leaders in the Church*, 53.

3. Fiorenza, *In Memory of Her*, 177.

4. Swidler, *Biblical Affirmations of Woman*, 296.

the nature of the greeting suggests greater independence." They go on to say that Apphia may have been a patron of the community as well.[5]

According to one source, "In the Greek church, November 22 is sacred to her (Apphia's) memory."[6] A tradition also exists to the effect that Apphia was a martyr. "She was stoned to death with Philemon, Onesimus and Archippus in the reign of Nero."[7] Another scholar says, somewhat dogmatically, "Of this Phrygian matron we know nothing more than can be learnt [sic] from this epistle (Philemon). The tradition or fiction which represents her as martyred together with her husband may be safely disregarded."[8]

I have raised the question with one of my colleagues in Church History concerning this date, and he confirmed the fact that it is sacred to Apphia's memory in the Greek Church; and that she *was* considered to have been a martyr. The fact that a date would be held sacred to her memory in this rather sizable sector of the church strongly suggests that she was neither an ordinary Christian nor mere wife of a church leader. The parallel addresses to Philemon, Apphia, and Archippus have been noted above. Given the above evidence I would suggest that all three were leaders of equal status in the church that met in Philemon's house. Whether a familial relationship existed among the three would be a moot point.

As a sort of postlude to the story of Apphia, I discovered something in the non-canonical work called the *Acts of Paul* that is most interesting to ponder. "And Apphia, the wife of Chrysippus, who was possessed by a demon, was healed by Paul."[9] The reliability of this tradition is unknown, and we cannot be certain that this refers to the same Apphia whom Paul addresses in Philemon, since this name is prominent in Phrygia.[10] Her association with Paul, however, creates at least the possibility that she is the same Apphia as in Philemon 2. If so, we would have to discount the idea that she was the wife of Philemon, since her husband is mentioned as

---

5. Kraemer and D'Angelo, *Women and Christian Origins*, 206.
6. The *International Standard Bible Encyclopaedia*, s.v. "Apphia."
7. Ibid.
8. Lightfoot, *Saint Paul's Epistles to the Colossians and to Philemon*, 308.
9. Hennecke and Schneemelcher, *New Testament Apocrypha*, II: 336.
10. See, for example, Marshall et al., eds., *The International Greek Testament Commentary, The Epistles to the Colossians and Philemon*; Allen, gen. ed., *2 Corithinans-Philemon*, 381: Lightfoot, *Saint Paul's Epistles to the Colossians and to Philemon*, 306–7. (Page citations are to the reprint edition.)

Apphia

Chrysippus. This, of course, raises other questions as to what had become of Chrysippus at the time Paul wrote Philemon, and there may be no way of answering such questions.

PART TWO

Unnamed Women

41

Manoah's Wife

Though she is never named, the story of Manoah's wife represents an extraordinary departure from the normal or expected. Not once, but twice, does she receive a divine visitor who informs her that she will have a son, and a very special one at that (Judg 13:5). After her first encounter with the strange visitor she informs Manoah her husband of the promise that she will bear a son. He then requests of the Lord that the divine visitor come again and teach him and his wife what to do for the boy who is to be born (Judg 13:8). The request is granted, and the visitor returns—but once again comes to the wife instead of to Manoah (Judg 13:9).

Bellis has aptly noted that "Although Manoah's wife is not named, she is clearly the stronger human character in this story. It is she who primarily interacts with the angel and she who recognizes the angel as an angel. The story makes Manoah look foolish, but his wife appears wise."[1] She further comments, "Manoah's wife is discerning, intelligent, and thoughtful. Manoah is obtuse. The differences between them lie not in supposedly gender-based approaches to seeing reality but in their individual gifts or lack thereof."[2] Exum echoes the same interpretation, noting that by denying to Manoah as much knowledge as she possesses the narrative shows the woman as the more important of the two and shows her to be more perceptive than Manoah.[3]

---

1. Bellis, *Helpmates Harlots Heroes*, 123.
2. Ibid., 124.
3. Exum, *Fragmented Women*, 64. After noting the more important role of Manoah's wife, however, Exum goes on to point out that this still serves patriarchal interests in that we see her only in the "safe" role of mother, without any hint of sexual desirability; not even the somewhat common Biblical phrase that "So-and-so knew his wife and she conceived." Cf. ibid., 65–66.

This time we encounter a woman who has a husband, but whose husband is placed in a secondary role. Obviously there must have been many details to this story that we do not possess. What little we do have places her in the independent role of receiving a revelation from God, which is only passed on to Manoah by his wife. That revelation included the fact that the son to be born would be a Nazarite from birth, with all that that required (Judg 13:5, 7). Only when Manoah (who finally gets his audience with the "angel of the Lord") asks what the boy's vocation will be does he receive this information (Judg 13:12–14).

Manoah's wife also proves herself to be the more perceptive and rational of the two in the events that followed. As Manoah was offering up a burnt offering the "angel of the Lord" ascended in the flame of the altar, causing both Manoah and his wife to fall on their faces to the ground (Judg 13:20). Manoah affirmed the ancient belief that because they had seen *God* (not an angel) they would surely die (Judg 13:22). His wife responded that if God had wanted to kill them he would not have accepted an offering from their hands (Judg 13:23).

Manoah's wife must have been a truly exceptional woman. Those of a more extreme feminist bent will quite naturally comment on the fact that she is not even given a name. Perhaps it is worth noting that her *story* could not be squelched. I, too, would like to have seen her given proper honor and mentioned by name, but, given the patriarchal culture of the time, it may be little short of miraculous that we have the story as it appears in the Bible. Perhaps her story was too important to the development of the Israelite people to be left out, even if her name was separated from that story.

42

The Heroine of Thebez

THIS WOMAN'S STORY CONSISTS of a single sentence embedded in a narrative of intrigue and struggle for power following the death of the judge Gideon (Jerub-baal). Abimelech, the son of Gideon by a maidservant (Judg 9:18), persuaded the people of Shechem to make him king and proceeded to wipe out all the male descendants of Gideon, seventy men in all (Judg 9:5). The only exception was Jotham, who managed to escape from Abimelech's hand (see Judg 9:5–21). After reigning for three years, Abimelech's relationship with the people of Shechem turned sour, and he marched against the city and destroyed it (Judg 9:23–45). Then, for reasons not specified in the text, Abimelech marched against the nearby city of Thebez and captured it. The leaders of Thebez and other citizens retreated to a strong tower in the center of the city. When Abimelech approached the tower, "A certain woman threw an upper millstone on Abimelech's head, crushing his skull" (Judg 9:54). Abimelech then ordered his armor bearer to pierce him through with his sword so it could not be said that a woman had killed him! Probably being killed by the hands of a woman was the most shameful death imaginable, especially to one who would have considered himself to be a great warrior.

The sentence above from Judges 9:53 is the sum total of this woman's story as it appears in the sacred text. The brevity of the statement fairly shouts a whole litany of questions at us. Where were the male warriors? Why was this woman allowed to be the one to climb to the top of the tower and throw the millstone at Abimelech? Was she the real leader of the community to whom the men were in the habit of deferring? Did the woman have a husband? If so, where was he when the battle was going on? The questions could go on and on—but the text gives us no answers. Though speculative, del Mastro's suggestion that the woman had tried more than once to reason with the men of the city and get them to take action before taking matters into her own hands is highly plausible.[1]

Once more we see a woman who is not defined by a husband or any other male. Despite the brevity of her story, she changed the course of Israel's history by her actions. As Winter has aptly noted, "The heroine of Thebez accomplished what warriors had failed to do, yet she is known to us simply as one of the countless women who wove their experience into the strong fabric of life during the time of the judges in Israel."[2] Like Manoah's wife, her story was too important not to be preserved, though both suffered the fate of namelessness.

---

1. del Mastro, *All the Women of the Bible*, 320–21.
2. Winter, *Heroine of Thebez*.

43

The Medium of En-dor

Down through the centuries the woman mentioned in 1 Samuel 28:7–25 has been tabbed the *witch* of En-dor. As we get the story in 1 Samuel, Saul had banished all such women from Israel. Samuel, upon whose advice Saul had heavily relied, had died; and the Lord was not answering Saul "either by dreams or by Urim or by prophets" (1 Sam 28:6). The bitter enemies of Israel, the Philistines, were encamped a short distance from the Israelite camp, and Saul was desperate for a message from the Lord. In his desperation he asks his servants to find a "medium" to whom he can go to ask about a message from God. He is told that there is a *baalath-'ob* (a woman who is a medium) in the village of En-dor. Saul goes to her and asks her to bring Samuel from the dead. Samuel appears and gives Saul a message, but it's one Saul did not want to hear. The message is that Israel will be delivered into the hands of the Philistines and that Saul and his sons will die the next day—and the kingdom will be given to David.

This is a strange story, to say the least, and it leaves us with more questions than answers. The woman of En-dor is obviously portrayed as a necromancer, but there may be more here than meets the eye. The Hebrew word *baalath* is the feminine form of the word *baal*, which means "lord" or "master." Hence, a proper translation would be something like "mistress." The word has clear connotations of authority. What does *baalath* mean in conjunction with the word *'ob*? Without going into a technical discussion, the latter seems to reflect an ancient belief that a Python or soothsaying demon sometimes lived in people, giving them the ability to foretell the future. The translators of the Greek version of the Jewish Scriptures rendered it *engastrimythos*, which literally means "having a myth (narrative, story, saying) in the womb or belly." Perhaps the best we can do is to affirm that the woman of En-dor was mistress of her house and was believed to have had a special gift that enabled her to communicate with the spirits of those who had died. The authenticity of the words from Samuel was confirmed fully by the events of the following days.

Does this woman deserve to be called a witch? On this issue I am very unsure. The usual words denoting witchcraft are largely absent from the text. Nunnally-Cox notes that "the woman is nowhere called witch. Yet over the centuries she has commonly been referred to as the 'witch of Endor.' The Authorized Version describes her as 'a woman that hath a familiar spirit'; the Revised Standard Version calls her a 'medium.' But the footnotes and page headings of these versions speak of 'the witch,' and many commentators label 1 Samuel 28:3–25 as belonging to the Witch of Endor."[1] These words from Nunnally-Cox give a fairly clear picture of the treatment that the woman from En-dor has received at the hands of both translators and commentators.

In light of the above, the treatment of this woman by the Jewish historian Flavius Josephus is fascinating. Josephus is not known for portraying women in a positive light, to put it mildly. Yet in this case he portrays the woman of En-dor as possessing not only the qualities of hospitality, compassion, and so on, which accorded with the highest ideals of Jewish ethics, but also the qualities held in highest esteem in the larger Greco-Roman world. In Josephus's account the woman of Endor is presented as a worthy example for all to emulate.[2] He clearly viewed her as anything but a witch. I will refrain from further comments on this issue, and will limit my comments to the more obvious implications of the text. This woman, whatever the nature of her supernatural abilities, was an independent woman who ordered her own life. We find no mention of a husband or other males to which she might have been subjected. She was also a woman of means—and a woman of compassion. When Saul received the message of Samuel, he fell on the ground in a state of complete exhaustion and devastation at the prediction that he and his sons would die the next day (1 Sam 28:20). The woman begged him to allow her to set some food before him to replenish his strength, but he refused at first. Finally she slaughtered a fattened calf that she had "in the house," then baked bread for Saul and his servants as well (1 Sam 28:24). Apparently two servants accompanied Saul at this point (1 Sam 28:8). They ate and went on their

---

1. Nunnally-Cox, *Foremothers*, 65.
2. *Antiquities* vi.xiv.3–4.

The Medium of En-dor

way. The fact that she had a fattened calf and that she baked bread for all of them indicates that she was not an ordinary poor widow, or anything of the sort. Bellis says she had servants, but I am unable to find this detail in the text.[3] Perhaps she has mistaken a reference to Saul's servants as a reference to the woman's servants. However, the slaughtering of a calf and baking of bread would appear to be more than a woman could accomplish alone. Perhaps we would be justified in concluding that she must have had servants to help her, even though the text is silent on this point.

---

3. Bellis, *Helpmates Harlots Heroes*, 142.

44

The Wise Woman of Tekoa

THIS WOMAN'S STORY IS found in 2 Samuel 14:2–20. The story behind her story is one of family dysfunction in the household of King David. One of his sons, Amnon, had raped his half-sister Tamar; and her brother Absalom had determined to avenge that rape. His plan consisted of inviting all of David's sons to a sheep-shearing festival. David responded that so many people would be burdensome to Absalom, and that he himself would therefore not come. Absalom then insisted that Amnon go with him. David was apparently suspicious and pointedly asked Absalom why he wanted Amnon to come with him (2 Sam 13:26). Absalom gave no direct answer, but kept insisting that Amnon come with him and his servants (2 Sam 13:27). David finally agreed. Absalom then instructed his servants that when Amnon's heart was "merry with wine" he would then give the command to kill him. After the servants carried out his command, all of David's other sons fled on their mules, expecting that any one of them could be next (2 Sam 13:29). Absalom himself, apparently expecting retribution from his father, fled to Geshur where he remained for three years (2 Sam 13:38).

David's army commander, Joab, noting the estrangement of David from his son Absalom, decided to do something about the situation. This is where the wise woman of Tekoa comes in. Joab instructed this woman to dress in mourning clothes and go to the king and pretend to have been mourning for many days (2 Sam 14:2). He also instructed her as to the specific things she should say to the king. She followed Joab's instructions and went to David, supposedly to ask for his help. She pretended that *she* had two sons, one of which killed the other, and was afraid the other son would be killed—and hence her husband's name would perish (2 Sam 14:7). Niditch has noted the similarities with the story of Cain and Abel and suggested that this may have provided a literary model for the contrived story that Joab instructed the woman to tell David.[1] When he heard the story, David assured her that he was willing to protect her son (2 Sam 14:11). In this story she was clearly setting David up. She then asked to speak a word to the king. Here she goes well beyond Joab's instructions. David gave her permission to speak, and she told him that he was guilty, in that he did not bring his estranged son Absalom back home (2 Sam 14:12-13). Carmody elaborates on this theme, saying, "We may note, first, that the woman accuses David of having planned 'such a thing' (the death of the best heir to the throne) 'against the people of God.' Several implications bristle in these phrases. 'Such a thing' is to be more interested in punishment, the letter of the law, than in mercy and good sense. It is to continue old ways of blood feud, a life for a life, that ill fit the existence created by the covenants (Mosaic and Davidic alike). 'The people of God' deserve better, should do better. God has not treated them according to strict laws of justice and vengeance. If God had, who could have survived?"[2] A few lines later Carmody continues, "One can almost see the woman raising a frail fist to threaten the king out of his obtuseness. Joab may have gotten her to play the role of provocateuse, but she has made it her own. Her verdict on the king—that, in his decision for her, he convicts himself—rings with authority. The wisdom attributed to her has produced a doughty self-confidence: she is sure of the role she is playing and can enact it with conviction."[3]

David somehow determined that Joab was behind all this, and the woman confirmed his suspicions (2 Sam 14:19). David then sent Joab to bring Absalom back to Jerusalem (although he sent Absalom to his own house and did not see his face for two years) [2 Samuel 14:28]. Parales notes that this woman performed the same role as had Nathan the prophet regarding David's adultery with Bathsheba (see above).[4]

On a first reading, this story appears to be about a woman who is completely controlled by the men of her society. It is true that she acts fully in accord with what Joab instructs her to say and do. Furthermore, she is subservient when she approaches David. Initially, it appears that patriarchy is alive and well. However, perhaps we should take a second look

1. Niditch, *Oral World and Written Word*, 19–20.
2. Carmody, *Biblical Women*, 45.
3. Ibid., 45–46.
4. Parales, *Hidden Voices*, 25; cf. John Carmody, Denise Lardner Carmody, and Robert L. Cohn, *Exploring the Hebrew Bible*, 45.

at this story. *Why* did Joab choose this woman to speak to David instead of doing so himself? Could it be that this unnamed woman had such a reputation for wise counsel that Joab knew she could accomplish what he could not? After all, Joab was David's army commander and surely was frequently in the king's presence. Joab could obviously have spoken to David personally about this matter. That he chose not to do so may tell us a great deal more about this wise woman from Tekoa than does the Biblical text. Another insight about this woman is contained in that text. She is described as a wise woman, using the same Hebrew word as for the wise woman of Abel Beth-maacah (below). Once more, when we look beneath the surface of her story, we find an independent woman who is not defined by a husband or any other male. Her reputation for wisdom must have been rather widely known, because Joab went to Tekoa from Jerusalem to find her. This was a distance of only about twelve miles; but in a day when there were no mechanical means of communication, I suggest that her reputation must have been renowned for it to reach from Tekoa to Jerusalem by word of mouth. Berquist has done an excellent job of evaluating this woman. "This woman was capable of complex and nuanced theology, and she had the courage to speak this sharp critique directly to the king. She went beyond Joab's deceit and taught the king about Yahweh's intentions for him. Her courage and her wisdom gave her power, and her power healed the king, if only for a while. The Tekoite woman's power was not destructive power; it was restorative, positive power, used effectively (even in defiance of Joab's guidance) to improve the situation and to proclaim her faith in God."[5] Brenner offers yet another evaluation:

> She has the presence of mind to seize upon a situation, judge it for herself, and manipulate it to her own advantage. These precisely are the qualities which made Joab choose her for this particular assignment. If we were to attempt a definition of this woman's wisdom (using our biblical text as it stands, and rejecting any knowledge which is external to it) we should arrive at the following conclusions. This "wise" woman can be commissioned to manipulate a person to act the way she wants him to. She achieves this by enlisting the person's cooperation instead of arousing his anger or animosity. She can be counted on for sensing undercurrents of emotions and opinions, and for utilizing them. She can adapt

---

5. Berquist, *Reclaiming Her Story*, 117. See also F. Scott Spencer, *Dancing Girls*, 83.

The Wise Woman of Tekoa

easily to changes in the atmosphere, and redirects these changes according to her purpose through improvisation. In short, she is adept in both rhetoric and psychology; her services can be commanded or hired (the text does not specify whether Joab did pay her) in order to mediate in, or influence the course of, personal and political disputes.[6]

Apparently this woman and the woman of Abel Beth-maacah (below) were the only ones in the Jewish Scriptures to be described as wise women (Heb *chakamah*).[7]

---

6. Brenner, *The Israelite Woman*, 35.

7. Brown, Driver and Briggs, *A Hebrew and English Lexicon of the Old Testament*, s.v. "Chakamah." Cf. Swidler, *Biblical Affirmations of Woman*, 89–90.

45

The Wise Woman of Abel Beth-maacah

THIS WOMAN'S STORY IS set during the time that David was consolidating his power as king. One Sheba, son of Bichri (2 Sam 20:1), had led a rebellion against David. Joab, the commander of David's army, had pursued Sheba to the city of Abel Beth-maacah. Because Sheba had taken refuge within the city walls, Joab's men set out to topple those walls (2 Sam 20:15). The (unnamed) wise woman calls out, apparently from the top of the city walls,[1] requesting Joab to come and speak to her. She then reminds Joab that people in times past had come to seek advice at Abel for the settling of disputes (2 Sam 20:18).[2] She charges Joab with "seeking to destroy a city, even a mother in Israel" (2 Sam 20:19). Joab replies that he is not bent on swallowing up or destroying anything, but only on punishing one who has raised his hand against King David. He says if she will deliver Sheba over to him he will depart from the city (2 Sam 20:21a). She then promises to throw Sheba's head over the wall. According to the NASB "Then the woman wisely came to all the people. And they cut off the head of Sheba the son of Bichri and threw it to Joab." I would prefer the translation, "Then the woman came to all the people in her wisdom and they cut off the head of Sheba son of Bichri and they threw it unto Joab." This translation is more accurate, in my judgment, and it places the emphasis on the wisdom of the woman herself, rather than the fact that she was wise to go to all the people. As Julia Beck has noted, judging from her "power of counsel in time of war, this woman appears to have wielded, at least locally, the power of a Deborah."[3] Grenz notes further that "this unnamed woman stands as an example of what Edmund Jacob

---

1. Cf. del Mastro, *All the Women of the Bible*, 408–9.
2. Cf. Brown, *Nameless Women of the Bible*, 54.
3. Unpublished research paper cited in Swidler, *Biblical Affirmations of Woman*, 90.

describes as 'a special class, distinct from prophets and priests ... who by their counsel have an active influence on the course of events.'"[4] Brenner further notes,

> The woman is widely respected: everybody listens attentively to what she has to say, from Joab to her fellow townspeople. She has authority and influence. After assessing the situation, she does not hesitate and gives Joab an immediate answer to his request. She is as good as her word: she convinces the assembly that it is imperative to comply with Joab's demands, and ensures that it [sic] is carried out. Therefore, it seems that she is no ordinary woman. She probably enjoys some kind of a unique status or reputation. Her position is such that she can approach the assembly (of which, traditionally, only males are members) and speak to it. This, even in times of a danger as great as the one described here, is quite extraordinary.[5]

The Greek translation of the Jewish Scriptures has some interesting variations from the Hebrew at this point. It reads, "And the woman entered in to all the people and she spoke to all the city in her wisdom; and *she* cut off the head of Sheba son of Bichri and *she* threw it to Joab" (emphasis mine).

Regardless of who cut off Sheba's head, clearly this unnamed woman took charge of the situation. By courageously confronting Joab, she saved the entire city from destruction. This is the same Joab who, without any apparent scruples, carried out David's orders to place Uriah in the thick of the battle and then withdraw from him so as to make sure he would be killed (see above); and who has just brutally murdered his own cousin Amasa (2 Sam 20:10).[6] She was taking her life in her hands by this confrontation. She was clearly a woman who commanded the respect of Joab, as well as all the people of her city. It is interesting to note that no male of Abel Beth-maacah plays any explicit role whatsoever. And, once Joab had Sheba's head in his possession, he was true to his word and departed from the city, along with all his soldiers.

---

4. Grenz with Muirkjesbo, *Women in the Church*, 66.
5. Brenner, *The Israelite Woman*, 36.
6. For the kinship of Joab and Amasa, see 1 Chr 2:16.

46

The Queen of Sheba

THIS WOMAN'S REMARKABLE STORY is found in 1 Kings 10:1-13 and, with minor variations, in 2 Chronicles 9:1-12. In Matthew 12:42 and the parallel in Luke 11:31 she is referred to as "the queen of the south." Sheba is a transliteration, rather than a translation of the Hebrew *Sheba*. Some confusion exists as to the exact area over which she was queen. The Jewish historian Josephus refers to her as queen of Ethiopia and Egypt at one point, then only as queen of Ethiopia at another.[1] Gesenius connects the name with Sabeans, and specifies the area as Arabia Felix, the southwest part of Arabia.[2] If Gesenius be correct, this might explain why Jesus refers to her as coming "from the ends of the earth" to hear Solomon (Matt 12:42, Luke 11:31).

Leaving aside the uncertainty concerning the area of her reign, we are told that the fame of Solomon had reached her, and that she came to visit Solomon to see for herself whether what she had heard was true. According to the text, she asked Solomon a variety of questions to test him, and he answered every one satisfactorily (1 Kgs 10:2-3; 1 Chr 9:1-2). The queen, upon seeing the splendor of Solomon's palace and all his wealth and servants, concluded that not half had been told her about him (1 Kgs 10:7; 1 Chr 9:6). She and Solomon exchanged extraordinarily expensive gifts. According to 1 Kings 10:13, "King Solomon gave to the queen of Sheba all her desire, which she requested, *besides what he gave her according to his royal bounty* (emphasis mine)." The Chronicler has

---

1. *Antiquities* viii.vi.v.

2. *Gesenius' Hebrew and Chaldee Lexicon*, s.v. "Sheba." William Whiston, in his translation of the works of Flavius Josephus, says, "That this queen of Sheba was a queen of Sabea in South Arabia, and not of Egypt and Ethiopia, as Josephus here asserts, is now generally agreed." See *Antiquities*, viii.vi.v, n. See also Theron Brown, *Nameless Women*, 66, n. For further discussion, see Bellis, *Helpmates Harlots Heroes*, 164.

modified this to read, "And King Solomon gave to the queen of Sheba all her desire which she requested besides *a return for* what she had brought to the king (1 Chr 9:12). The version in 1 Kings leaves the tantalizing question as to what it was that Solomon gave to her "besides what he gave her according to his royal bounty." According to an Abyssinian legend, the queen of Sheba bore a child by Solomon.[3] In a possible allusion to this legend Winters writes, "It is hard to determine the nature of the queen's relationship with Solomon. Given the size of Solomon's harem, his attraction to foreign women, and the queen's own magnetic personality, it is fair to suspect that this king and queen shared more than clever words."[4] Camp has referred to the account of the queen's encounter with Solomon as "lady wisdom" come to test Solomon who passes the test, but as also concealing only partially an erotic subtext.[5]

Evaluation of this woman must begin by affirming that she was an independent, highly intelligent woman who did not hesitate to check out rumors she had heard, even when those rumors concerned the king of another country. Josephus says of her, "There was then a woman, queen of Egypt and Ethiopia; she was inquisitive into philosophy, and one that on other accounts also was to be admired."[6] Brown writes, "It is fair to think of her as a woman who had studied much, and had found many problems, social, economical, [sic] political and moral, that she could not solve to her satisfaction, and when she came to the famous Hebrew king 'to prove him with hard questions' we believe it was to learn something of solid and lasting value to herself rather than merely to match wits with him and play a game of riddles—as oriental monarchs were so fond of doing with each other."[7] Stanton aptly comments, "Solomon did not suggest to the queen that she was out of her sphere, that home duties, children and the philosophy of domestic life were the proper subjects for her consideration; but he talked with her as one sovereign should with another."[8] There is no hint in this story of a husband or any other man of her native country who played any role in her life. Winter makes the significant

---

3. *International Standard Bible Encyclopaedia*, s.v. "Queen of Sheba."
4. Winter, *Queen of Sheba*.
5. As cited in Bellis, *Helpmates Harlots Heroes*, 164.
6. *Antiquities* viii.vi.v.
7. Theron Brown, *Nameless Women*, 65–66.
8. Stanton, *The Woman's Bible*, II:65.

comment that "The Queen of Sheba was a woman of power and influence, prosperity and prestige, who showed women of biblical tradition another way of being female."[9]

---

9. Winter, *Queen of Sheba*.

47

The Shunammite Woman

THIS WOMAN'S STORY APPEARS in 2 Kings 4:8–37 in the context of the ministry of Elisha, successor to the great prophet Elijah. She is described at the beginning as a "prominent woman" (2 Kgs 4:8). The Greek translation of the Jewish Scriptures refers to her as a *megalē* ("great") woman. The Hebrew version fully supports this translation, describing her as a *gedolah* woman. She has a husband, to be sure, but he is a completely "silent partner" in the story. Only the woman speaks or acts.

As the story unfolds, the prophet Elisha passed over to Shunem where this woman lived, and she persuaded him to eat food each time he passed that way (2 Kgs 4:8). She then spoke to her husband, saying she recognized Elisha to be a man of God, and proposed building a walled chamber on top of their house for him, complete with bed, table, and chair, so that any time Elisha came by he could stay there (2 Kgs 4: 9–10). One day Elisha sent his servant Gehazi to call the woman and ask if they could do anything for her, such as mentioning her to the king or the army commander (2 Kgs 4:13). The woman answered, "I live among my own people," apparently saying she was not interested in hobnobbing with royalty or highly placed officials! Elisha then asked Gehazi what they should do for her. Gehazi answered that she had no son, and that her husband was old, thus suggesting that giving her a son might be appropriate (2 Kgs 4:14). So Elisha called the woman and told her she would embrace a son in the next year (2 Kgs 4:15–16). The woman was skeptical, but she did bear a son (2 Kgs 4:16–17). After the child was "grown," he came in from reaping grain, complaining of his head. Considering the fact that he had been out in the open field for several hours in what would have been a rather hot time of the year causes one to think of sun stroke. Probably no one at that time knew anything about sun stroke, only that he complained of his head while out in the fields. He died shortly thereafter, and his mother took him and laid him on Elisha's bed.

Some of the details here are a bit strange, and call for some explanation. In 4:18 the son is said to have been grown, yet he dies after sitting on his mother's lap, apparently for an extended period of time. In addition, she would have had to climb a flight of stairs carrying his body in order to place him on Elisha's bed. It is doubtful whether she could have done this with a fully grown man's body. The Hebrew text uses the word *yigdal* here, which may be translated "he became great" or simply that "he grew." The Greek text uses the verb *hadrunomai*, which may be translated "he became mature" or "he increased." However, the Greek text also refers to the son as a *paidirion*, which is a diminutive form of a Greek word for child (*pais*), and hence would naturally be rendered as "little child." Furthermore, it was another *paidirion* who was instructed to take him to his mother (4:19). It appears that the evidence best supports the idea that the son had come to some level of maturity, but was still a child. Perhaps we should note here that maturity in the ancient world was considerably different, that is, it came at a much earlier age, than in the modern world. Having said all this, I will venture the "educated guess" that the son had matured sufficiently to go out into the fields with the reapers, but may have been no more than 8–10 years old, or perhaps even younger. del Mastro refers to the child as being five years old, but without giving any evidence for her conclusion.[1]

After the child died, his mother called for a donkey and, along with a servant, went to find Elisha (2 Kgs 4:18–24). She found him on Mount Carmel and, in her distress, took hold of Elisha's feet. Gehazi wanted to push her away, but Elisha saw that she was troubled, and inquired as to what was wrong (2 Kgs 4:25–28). When Elisha learned that her son had died (although this detail is left out of the text!), he sent Gehazi to lay his staff on the son's face, apparently in an attempt to restore him to life (2 Kgs 4:29). The woman then vows that she will not leave Elisha, apparently demanding that he come to her house in person (2 Kgs 4:30). As Winter puts it, "She stood in the background, bound by formality, when the prophet promised her a child, but she pushed forward, forcefully, to confront the

---

1. del Mastro, *All the Women of the Bible*, 387.

prophet directly when the child he had promised her died. *She challenged the prophet and won*" (emphasis mine).²

When he came to the house, Gehazi reported that the lad had not come back to life (2 Kgs 4:31). Elisha then, after praying to the Lord, gave the son mouth-to-mouth resuscitation, and brought him back to life (2 Kgs 4:32–35). He then called the woman and gave her back her son. (The similarity to the story of Elijah's resuscitation of the son of the widow of Zarephath as found in 1 Kings 17:17–24 is rather striking.)

This woman appears once more in the narrative. At Elisha's urging she took her household and went to the land of the Philistines for seven years, because of a famine in Judah. Nothing is said of her husband this time and, since he was described earlier as being old, the presumption is that he had died;³ although the Biblical text is silent on this. When she returned she appealed to the king for the restoration of her property and, with Elisha's help, she received back not only her house and field but all that her field had produced in the seven years that she was absent (2 Kgs 8:1–6; cf., Theron Brown, *Nameless Women of the Bible*, 106).

This woman's story differs considerably from the two wise women (above), in that she did have a husband. Her life is clearly not defined by that husband, however, and at every point it is she who takes the initiative. As Bellis has noted, "The Shunammite woman is a strong character; her husband, [*sic*] a weak one."⁴ Stanton's description of her may go beyond what the text will support at some points, but contains considerable truth, in my judgment. "She was a very discreet and judicious woman and her husband had always entrusted everything to her management. She was devout and conscientious and greatly enjoyed the godly conversation of the prophet. She was known in the city as a great and good woman."⁵ Brown says of her, "We have a right to believe that she was a lady of wealth and social distinction, and an example of hospitality and benevolence. All that we know of her indicates that she was a devout worshipper of Jehovah, and loved the society of holy people; and it is fair to infer that her husband was of the same spirit."⁶ We might concur with all that Brown

---

2. Winter, *Shunammite Woman*.
3. Cf. Theron Brown, *Nameless Women of the Bible*, 104.
4. Bellis, *Helpmates Harlots Heroes*, 173.
5. Stanton, *The Woman's Bible*, II:79.
6. Theron Brown, *Nameless Women of the Bible*, 95.

says, but this falls far short of capturing the spirit of this intelligent, resourceful, and decisive woman.

In his concluding remarks Brown writes of the Shunammite woman, "None of all the more glorious females on the roll of ancient Hebrew wifehood, motherhood and queenhood ever more justly earned a place for her picture in the sacred cabinet of nobility and virtue than this high-minded daughter of Issachar; and none of all the nameless more richly deserved a name. Were we to invent one for her it would be Asherel, 'Blessed of God.'"[7] His remarks may be somewhat exaggerated, but I would certainly concur in his statement that she richly deserves a name.

---

7. Ibid., 107.

48

The Wife of Isaiah

As I have noted earlier, this is one of only five women in the Jewish Scriptures to be given the title of prophet. She is the only unnamed woman to be given this title. Her mention in the Jewish Scriptures consists of a bare mention in Isaiah 8:3 where she gives birth to a son whose name is to be a sign (Isa 8:18) to Israel of the imminent devastation of Israel by the armies of Assyria.

This female prophet has been given very little notice by scholars. I perused six different Bible dictionaries, and found almost nothing beyond the bare fact that the prophet Isaiah was married. Only one of the six used the word prophetess at all, and I found no discussion whatever even in that one reference of any prophetic function being implied by the title. This silence in and of itself speaks volumes. In Brenner's words, "By definition, prophetic activities ascribed to women should not be different from those attributed to their male counterparts."[1] Parales comments further, "The writers of the Old Testament mentioned her (Isaiah's wife) and other women prophets without bringing any attention to the fact that they were women; it must have been generally assumed that God chose women as well as men to be mouthpieces for God and proclaimers of truth."[2] Murphy expresses a similar opinion. "Four women are explicitly given the title 'prophet'—Miriam, Huldah, Noadiah, and the wife of Isaiah; the unremarkable manner in which the Bible mentions the status of these women suggests that the role of prophet was an established one."[3]

Patriarchal interpreters are fond of arguing that the word "prophetess" in Isaiah 8:3 means nothing more than that she was the wife of

1. Brenner, *The Israelite Woman*, 57.
2. Parales, *Hidden Voices*, 23.
3. Murphy, *The Word according to Eve*, 101. Why Murphy has left Deborah out of his list is inexplicable.

a prophet. Watts refers to this interpretation, and then responds by saying, "'[P]rophetess' must refer to Isaiah's wife. Wildberger is right (contra Duhm and Proksch) that the title does not simply mean 'a prophet's wife.' Rather it is understood that she, like Hulda (*sic*) [2 Kgs 22:14] served as a prophet in the Temple as well as participating in the sign by birthing a son."[4] Winter makes some illuminating comments: "We do not know if this woman was indeed a prophet, if she left any writings, if she uttered any oracles. We do not know if some of her husband's prophesies were really hers. Perhaps her writings remained unpublished or unpopular because she was female or because her husband's words overshadowed hers. Or perhaps they found their way into Isaiah's book. It is generally accepted that the Book of Isaiah was not written entirely by one author. The female images in the text might have come from her."[5]

---

4. Hubbard and Barker, gen. eds., *Isaiah 1–33*, 113.
5. Winter, *Wife of Isaiah*.

49

The Idealized Woman of Proverbs 31

IN CHOOSING TO DEAL with this theoretical woman I may well draw the negative criticism that I have deviated from my thesis. My reasoning is that this idealized woman reflects sufficient deviations from the normal role of women in the Jewish Scriptures that she deserves to be considered along with the actual, historical women. Further, if this idealized woman did not reflect that such women actually existed in Israelite society, I consider it highly unlikely that this passage would have found its way into the canon. (I would concede that this might be a composite picture, with no single individual woman embodying all the traits mentioned here.)

I will begin with some very interesting matters of translation. (This discussion will of necessity be somewhat technical, so any reader who has no background in Hebrew or Greek is free to skip this paragraph and go on to the next.) The ancient translations rendered the opening question of Proverbs 31:10 as, "Who can find a virtuous woman?" My first surprise came when I looked at the Hebrew text and noted that "virtuous" was the translation of the Hebrew *chayil*. When I looked this word up in Gesenius's lexicon to confirm whether or not I had the right definition in mind, the first four definitions I found were "strength, power, might (especially warlike), valour" [*sic*].[1] This all seemed to be fairly remote from the idea of mere virtue! My next step was to look at the Greek translation of the Jewish Scriptures. Here my surprise was even greater. The translators of the Greek Bible had used the adjective *andreias* to translate *chayil*. *Andreias* is the adjective form of the Greek word for man! Hence the natural translation would be, "Who can find a *manly* woman?" We're getting farther and farther from the idea of virtue! I looked at the three passages listed by Gesenius where *chayil* had been translated "virtuous,"

---

1. *Gesenius' Hebrew and Chaldee Lexicon*, s.v. *chayil*.

and found that the Greek translators had used *andreias* in Proverbs 12:4 and 31:10, and *dynamis* (which is the root of the English word "dynamite") in Ruth 3:11. Clearly the translators of the Jewish Scriptures into Greek thought the word meant power or strength! Perhaps these facts explain to a large degree the great latitude of readings in the English translations. Bellis renders the question, "A capable wife, who can find?"[2] as does the NRSV. Berquist prefers, "Who can find a strong woman?"[3] NASB reads, "An excellent wife, who can find." RSV reads, "A good wife, who can find?" The REV has the same translation, except for word order. The NIV reads, "A wife of noble character who can find?" Blankenhorn, Browning, and Van Leeuwen follow this reading.[4] The KJV has, "Who can find a virtuous woman?" Murphy renders the question, "A woman of valor, who can find?"[5] Swidler has the variation, "A perfect wife—who can find her?"[6] Yee argues that "woman of substance" is the preferred translation.[7] We see in this sampling of translations the absence of any idea of strength or power in all but one.

Reading the question at Proverbs 31:10 as, Who can find a woman of power? Or, Who can find a woman of strength (or valor)? gives a totally different slant on the entire passage that follows. This is no mere virtuous housewife, but a woman who possesses and exercises power and strength. She obviously does not neglect traditional wifely duties, but adds to them numerous functions that normally only males carried out. Let me single out first some of the former, then some of the latter, from Proverbs 31:11–31.[8]

This woman has the complete trust of her husband (v. 11). She searches for wool and flax and keeps herself and her family appropriately clothed (vv. 13, 19, 21–22). She arises before daybreak to feed both her family and her servants (v. 15). She is always concerned with her house-

---

2. Bellis, *Helpmates Harlots Heroes*, 197.

3. Berquist, *Reclaiming Her Story*, 136.

4. Blankenhorn, Browning, and Van Leeuwen, eds., *Does Christianity Teach Male Headship?* 84.

5. Metzger, gen. ed., *Proverbs*, 243.

6. Swidler, *Biblical Affirmations of Woman*, 126.

7. Yee, *Poor Banished Children of Eve*, 151.

8. I would like to give due credit at this point to Bilezikian, *Beyond Sex Roles*, for opening my eyes to the presence of many of the functions normally reserved for males in this passage.

The Idealized Woman of Proverbs 31

hold and is always at work to see that their needs are met (v. 27). Both husband and children praise her for these things (vv. 28–29).

Interspersed with these "wifely" duties we also find a woman who independently purchases real estate (v. 16a). From her independent wealth she plants a vineyard (v. 16b). She has a rigorous exercise program to increase her strength (v. 17). She is an entrepreneur who both produces and sells various items of clothing (v. 24). Her real clothing, however, is strength and dignity (v. 25). She is a teacher of wisdom and kindness (v. 26). As Keener notes, in an obviously understated manner, "This woman does not spend most of her time at home 'rearing the children.'"[9]

Admittedly, some of these verses could be read in either fashion. For example, the metaphor of bringing food from afar like merchant ships could be read as attesting to her aptitude for grocery shopping, or as indicating that, in her capacity as a businesswoman, she imported the finest of foods.[10] Extending her hand to the poor (v. 20) could imply merely giving handouts to the poor, or it could refer to her creating charitable organizations for this function.

Although I would not argue that this passage, or any other in the Jewish Scriptures, is free of patriarchy, I do argue that we find a great deal more in this passage. We find a picture of womanhood that is by and large at variance with the traditional idea of womanhood in that day.[11] I would argue that these verses demonstrate that in ancient Israelite society there was a place for women, however exceptional, who possessed "manly" qualities and, as I have suggested earlier, it may be in the exceptions that we find clearest evidence of divine inspiration. This is one way of dealing with the obviously ambivalent picture of woman that we find here.[12] Belleville highlights the ambivalence by first saying, "In Proverbs 31 the woman worth far more than rubies is a wise hardworking entrepreneur

---

9. Keeener, *Paul, Women and Wives*, 227.

10. Cf. Scanzoni & Hardesty, *All We're Meant to Be*, 285.

11. The wisdom literature is notoriously difficult to date. The final form of our book of Proverbs probably belongs to the time of Ezra, shortly after the Jews' return from captivity in Babylon. The content at some points probably goes back to the time of Solomon. Hence we may have a time span of c. 922 BCE to the fifth century BCE. My argument is that the picture of womanhood in Proverbs 31 is exceptional to any known view of womanhood in ancient Israel during this period. For further discussion of the dating of Proverbs, see Anderson, *Understanding the Old Testament*, 575–82.

12. For further reference to the ambivalence in this text see Yee, *Poor Banished Children of Eve*, 151–52.

who successfully juggles a family, a business, and a concern for the poor and needy of her community." She then goes on to say, "The seemingly liberated woman in Proverbs 31 still spins thread, manages her household, and cares for and instructs her children."[13] Bilezikian summarizes the picture in these words: "The mixture of negative and positive elements make of the old covenant a time of compromise between the pressures of the creation ideal and of the fall."[14] A further reflection of the ambivalence is found in the statements of feminists Denise Lardner Carmody and Alice Ogden Bellis in contrast to womanist Ella Pierson Mitchell. Carmody argues, "Even at its moments of high praise, the Bible reflects a man's world."[15] Bellis, in commenting on Proverbs 30:31, says, "Charm is not always deceitful, and a good wife doesn't have to be plain. Underlying these verses is the same fear of woman that we have seen throughout."[16] Mitchell, on the other hand, without denying that the male is the dominant figure (in Proverbs 31:10–31), asserts that "this book . . . proposes that women engage in business, to an extent not found anywhere else."[17] Parales says pointedly, "She was known for her wisdom (v. 26) and did not behave as a silent, submissive wife. She was a businesswoman involved in farming, manufacturing, and real estate. She made major financial decisions and ran her family's household, a situation that placed the power of the household in her hands."[18] In a similar vein Scanzoni and Hardesty write, "The picture in Proverbs 31 is not that of a 'clinging vine' or 'helpless female,' but rather of a mature woman of good business sense, capable of wise thought and management, resourceful, responsible, and highly esteemed by her husband who places his whole trust in her."[19]

Berquist has appropriately noted three basic reactions to the poem of Proverbs 31. The first two are praise and opposition, both of which we have noted above. The third reaction is that the poem asks too much from women. He then affirms the validity of all three reactions. In summary,

13. Belleville, *Women Leaders and the Church*, 83.
14. Bilezikian, *Beyond Sex Roles*, 78.
15. Denise Lardner Carmody, *Biblical Woman*, 73.
16. Bellis, *Helpmates Harlots Heroes*, 197. Cf. Swidler, *Biblical Affirmations of Woman*, 126.
17. Cited in Bellis, *Helpmates Harlots Heroes*, 198. Cf. Fiorenza, *In Memory of Her*, 109.
18. Parales, *Hidden Voices*, 28.
19. Scanzoni & Hardesty, *All We're Meant to Be*, 284.

he says, "Perhaps the poem reaches its greatest usefulness if conceived as a list of options and possibilities.... Within this interpretation, the list of Proverbs 31:10–31 may be able to energize women's self-determination and actualizing activity, without limiting roles, subordinating women to men, or overworking women." I would highly commend this usage of the poem.

50

The Samaritan Woman

THIS UNNAMED SAMARITAN WOMAN'S story is contained in John 4:7–42. Jesus initiated a conversation with her by asking her for a drink of water (v. 7). She proved to be a woman of spunk by challenging Jesus's request and informing him that Jews had no dealings with Samaritans.[1] After some conversation about water that is permeated with typical Johannine misunderstanding over "living water," and the request that he give her this water, Jesus invites her to call her husband and come back to the well (vv. 10–16). The woman replied that she had no husband (v. 17a). Jesus replied that she had spoken the truth, because she had had five husbands, and the one she had now was not *her* husband (vv. 17b–18).[2] An ancient and popular interpretation here suggests that the woman was sexually immoral, going from one man to another. As Schottroff notes, "male exegetes (and a few female interpreters as well) read the biography of the Samaritan woman as a story of sexual lust and unbridled passion."[3] Nowhere does the text say anything of the sort, however. Women were basically property at this point in history, and this woman could have been passed on from one man to another without having any choice in the matter. Though unlikely, the possibility exists that the law of levirate marriage led to her being wed to five brothers, with each marriage

---

1. The Greek text invites either the understanding that Jews and Samaritans were hostile to one another (which was assuredly true) and had no dealings whatever with each other, or that they did not use common vessels such as drinking vessels. Examination of several English translations will clearly reflect these two possibilities.

2. For centuries some interpreters have argued for an allegorical interpretation of the five husbands as symbolizing the five gods allegedly worshipped by the Samaritans (Cf. F. Scott Spencer, *Dancing Girls*, 81). We may safely leave such interpretation aside, in that there is absolutely nothing in the text to indicate that "husband" means anything except husband.

3. Schottroff, "Important Aspects of the Gospel for the Future," 209.

The Samaritan Woman

taking place after one brother died. The likelihood that this woman bore no moral blame for her situation is enhanced by the fact that nowhere in the text does Jesus say anything about her sin, unlike the story of the woman taken in adultery in John 7:53—8:11.[4] Stanton's assertion that "The woman could not understand Jesus' words because she had no conviction of sin nor desire for a purer, better life" are without any foundation in the text.[5] Getty-Sullivan perpetuates the popular inference that the woman was sexually promiscuous, saying, "She comes alone to the well at noon because she has been ostracized by more respectable women. She has had five husbands; everyone would know that about her."[6] This is a possibility, but is far from being demonstrable from the text. The possibility that her situation and workload forced her to come to the well several times during the day is just as likely.[7] Parales is much more sympathetic with the woman. She says,

> Because men could divorce their wives but women could not leave their husbands, she may well have been abandoned or divorced, or the men may all have died. Jesus was aware of her losses and her current life situation. She may have chosen simply to live with the sixth man because a sixth marriage may have been too much for her to bear. In any case, it is unlikely she was the town harlot, as tradition has made her out to be, because the townspeople listened to her when she came to tell them about Jesus. They would have laughed at her if she had a reputation for prostitution. Her reputation must have been intact enough for the Samaritan villagers to take her seriously.[8]

The next development is that the woman expresses the insight that Jesus is a prophet and poses the question to him of the proper place to worship (vv. 19-24). To properly appreciate this question a bit of geographical and Biblical information is necessary. Jacob's well lay at the foot of Mt. Gerizim, the traditional mount of blessing (cf. Deut 11:29). When the Israelites returned from Babylonian captivity the Samaritans offered to help them rebuild their temple, but were refused with a testy, "You have nothing in common with us in building a house to our God; but we our-

---

4. Cf. F. Scott Spencer, *Dancing Girls*, 91.
5. Stanton, *The Woman's Bible*, II:140.
6. Getty-Sullivan, *Women in the New Testament*, 95.
7. Cf. F. Scott Spencer, *Dancing Girls*, 88.
8. Parales, *Hidden Voices*, 41.

selves will together build to the Lord God of Israel, as King Cyrus, the king of Persia has commanded us" (Ezra 4:3). After the lapse of an indefinite number of years the Samaritans built a temple on Mount Gerizim.[9] With this in mind, the woman in effect was saying to Jesus, "You Jews have your temple in Jerusalem and you say that is where God dwells; we Samaritans have our temple on Mount Gerizim, and we say that is where God dwells: which one of us is correct?" Jesus's answer is that God is spirit (and hence gender-neutral, by the way) and place is no longer relevant. The woman then states her belief in a Messiah who would explain all things to the people. Jesus's reply may or may not indicate his acceptance of the role of that Messiah.[10] The Greek text has only, *Egō eimi, ho lalōn soi.* ("I am, the one speaking to you") Since "I am" is the name of God as revealed to Moses at the burning bush (Exod 3:14), Jesus was clearly identifying himself with God as revealed to Moses.[11] It could therefore be translated, "I Am (is) the one speaking to you."[12] The identification with the name of God as revealed to Moses is probably the primary significance, although I would not want to rule out the possibility that it may also have been an affirmation of Jesus as Messiah.[13]

9. It has been asserted by some that the Samaritan temple had been destroyed by John Hyrcanus sometime between 128 and 107 BCE (see, e.g. Getty-Sullivan, *Women in the New Testament*, 95; *Black's Bible Dictionary*, s.v. "Gerizim": *The International Standard Bible Encyclopaedia*, s.v. "Gerizim." The latter cites Josephus as his authority, but Josephus only says that Hyrcanus captured Shechem and Gerizim and the Cutheans who dwelt at or around the temple which resembled the one in Jerusalem. (See *Antiquities*, xii.ix.i; *Bellum* i.ii.vi.) Dr. Howard Clark Kee, in personal communication with me about fifteen years ago, asserted that he had supervised the archaeological dig on Mt. Gerizim, and that there was clearly a foundation to the Samaritan temple datable to the first century of the Common Era. Schottroff, citing Eusebius, says the Samaritan temple was destroyed by Titus and Hadrian, thus supporting the idea that the temple was still there during the lifetime of Jesus (Schottroff, "Important Aspects of the Gospel for the Future," 210).

10. Contra Carmody, *Biblical Woman*, 104; McKinlay, *Gendering Wisdom the Host*, 189: Parales, *Hidden Voices*, 41, et al.

11. Cf. also the last statement in Isa 45:18, "I am the Lord, and there is none else." The Greek text has, *Egō eimi, kai ouk estin eti* ("I am, and there is no other"). For further discussion, see McKinlay, *Gendering Wisdom the Host*, 197–99.

12. Cf. Harrington, ed., *The Gospel of John*, 130–31.

13. The "I am" sayings in the Fourth Gospel make an interesting study in and of themselves. The phrase appears on the lips of Jesus more than forty times in this Gospel. The sayings are fairly evenly divided between just the phrase "I am" as found at John 4:24 and the phrase with a predicate such as, "I am the light of the world," "I am the good shepherd," etc.

The Samaritan Woman

The next development is that the disciples come on the scene and marvel that he is talking with a woman (v. 27), but they were not about to challenge Jesus on this issue![14] The Samaritan woman then went back into the city and invited the *men* to come and see a man who told her everything she ever did. She then posed the question, *mēti houtos estin ho Christos?* ("This is not the Messiah, is it?") [vss. 28-29]. Carmody's words are worth quoting at some length.

> In this context, the woman's words "He told me all that I ever did" strike a responsive chord. Jesus had clarified the woman's life story. He had helped her structure her time, see where she had been and where she could be going. And though the woman may initially have been struck by his insight into her having been much married, it seems likely she soon became more interested in salvation: where to find the Messiah. Jesus was offering her a new interpretation of her possibilities. She need not think of herself as a being condemned to haul water and pleasure men. She could be a witness to salvation, a sharer and proclaimer of great good news. In offering her this new set of possibilities, this fresh way of defining herself, Jesus was gambling that she had the wherewithal to catch his drift, the gumption to make a change. He was not disappointed. The woman is in the Gospel of John not simply to occasion a couple of speeches about water, food, and messiahship. She is in the gospel as a model of faith.[15]

The men responded by coming to hear Jesus for themselves (v. 30). We are told that many of the Samaritans believed in Jesus because of the testimony of this woman (v. 39). Jesus was invited to spend some time in Samaria and remained there for two days.[16] Many more of the Samaritan men believed in Jesus, affirming that they no longer believed only because of the testimony of this woman, but had found out for themselves that he is the Savior of the world (vv. 41-42).

Fiorenza suggests that the woman's dialogue with Jesus has implications beyond this specific woman: "The dramatic dialogue is probably based on a missionary tradition that ascribed a primary role to a woman

---

14. Cf. Fiorenza, *In Memory of Her*, 326.
15. Carmody, *Biblical Women*, 105.
16. This, by the way, is the only hint in any of the Gospels of a mission of Jesus to the Samaritans. As noted above, the book of Acts places this mission well after the ascension of Jesus (see Acts 8:5-25).

missionary in the conversion of the Samaritans."[17] By contrast, in the book of Acts, Philip the Evangelist is the first to preach to the Samaritans (Acts 8:5). The latter places the Samaritan mission well after the time of the human Jesus. We again need to remind ourselves that we are not getting anything like a complete story on this issue; or any other, for that matter.

This story presents us with a woman who in some sense has a man in her life, but the text gives us no clue as to the exact nature of the relationship. Whatever may have been her relationship with the man (v. 18) she clearly acts independently of him. She is not afraid to challenge Jesus on the issue of Jews vs. Samaritans, nor is she hesitant to enter into dialogue with him on matters of theology. When she recognizes Jesus as a prophet, and possibly as the Messiah, she does not go to the man in her life to ask what she should do, but goes immediately to the men of her city and announces her encounter with Jesus, with its intimation that he just might be the Messiah. (In fact, the man in her life is silenced in this story and plays no part whatever beyond the bare mention by Jesus. We have become accustomed, unfortunately, to this treatment of women, but seldom is a man the victim of silence and namelessness. The husband of the Shunnamite Woman is another such exception.) The men take her testimony seriously and come to Jesus to find out for themselves who he is. This is remarkable, given the prevailing notion of the day that the testimony of women was not accepted as valid, at least in most Jewish circles. Swidler suggests that this text indicates that a higher value was placed upon women's testimony among Samaritans than among the Jews.[18] Reinhartz notes that this woman's actions make her an apostle and identifies her as one of those characterized as "one who sows" in this Gospel (v. 37).[19] Eisen notes that Origen of Alexandria characterized this woman as both an apostle and an evangelist, and that Theophylact (c. 1050–1108 CE) had also called her an apostle. Theophylact further expanded the title by referring to her as "anointed with priesthood" and as teacher of the entire city.[20] The writings of these ancient authors imply that this woman was far more important in Christian history than anything for which the text gives her credit. How we wish this woman could tell her story in its entirety!

17. Fiorenza *In Memory of Her*, 327.
18. Swidler, *Biblical Affirmations of Woman*, 189–90.
19. Adela Reinhartz, "Women in the Johannine Community," 21–22. Cf. also Getty-Sullivan, *Women in the New Testament*, 99.
20. Eisen, *Women Officeholders in Early Christianity*, 50.

51

The Woman and the Unjust Judge

THIS WOMAN'S STORY IS found in an unusual parable of Jesus contained in Luke 18:1–8. Obviously this is a hypothetical woman, but because Jesus's parables usually depicted realistic pictures of life in ancient Palestine, I believe we are justified in assuming that his hearers could have imagined such a woman as actually existing. As Jesus told the parable, a poor and helpless widow came to a judge who is described as "not fearing God and having no concern for human beings" to ask for his help (vv. 2–3). Despite the claims of Schottroff and others, we are not told the precise nature of the help the woman is seeking or who her adversary is; we only know that she needs help with an "opponent" and needs "legal protection" (v. 5). (Schottroff's contention that the opponent was a man who undermined the economic foundation of her life should have been preceded by the word "probably" or "possibly.")[1] At first the judge refuses to do anything, but later reconsiders and gives the widow the help she is seeking. For this, "She is commended by Jesus for her popularly tagged 'masculine' traits of aggressiveness and stick-toitiveness [sic]."[2] In the redaction of Luke this appears as a lesson in persistent prayer (vv. 6–8). However, as Dornisch notes, "It is easy to see today's parallels of those who are poor, especially poor women, who generally lack legal recourse, who often are given the 'run around,' and who are easily oppressed by bureaucratic and legal systems."[3]

Verse five presents some interesting possibilities of translation. The NASB translates, "yet because this woman bothers me, I will give her legal protection, lest by continually coming she wear me out." KJV, NIV, TEV,

---

1. See Schottroff, *Lydia's Impatient Sisters*, 101 and the sources she cites. Cf. Swidler, *Biblical Affirmations of Woman*, 166.
2. Ibid., 166.
3. Dornisch, *A Woman Reads the Gospel of Luke*, 187.

RSV, LNT, NEB, Rheims New Testament, and NRSV have slight variations of this translation; all indicate that the judge is afraid the woman will keep coming to him so frequently that it would "weary" him. Philips reads, "else her continual visits will be the death of me!" The NAB, however, translates the last phrase of this verse, "lest she finally come and *strike* me" (emphasis mine). The Amplified Bible has "lest she give me intolerable annoyance *and* wear me out by her continual coming *or* at the last she come and rail on me *or* assault me *or* strangle me." These last two translations differ dramatically from the others. In them the judge fears this woman might punch him out! At issue here is the Greek verb *hupōpiazō*. Its only other usage in the Christian Testament is at 1 Corinthians 9:27, where Paul speaks of "buffeting" (NASB) his body and making it his slave. If we accept the reading of the NAB and translate *hupōpiazō* as striking, a rather amusing picture results. Here is a macho, powerful judge known for his fearlessness, even of God, afraid that if he does not help this poor widow she will punch him out! Obviously, no man in his position could think of striking back physically against a "mere" woman, so reading the text in this fashion would give fully adequate reasons for the judge to give in to the woman's request.

Once again we find a story of a woman who would not settle for her lot in a corrupt human society. She refused to take no for an answer. She aggressively sought and found the help she needed from a man who did not want to help her. I realize fully that I am subject to the charge that I have created a real woman out of a hypothetical one, and that this woman may not have resembled any real woman in Israelite society of the time of Jesus. I doubt, however, that Jesus created this parable *ex nihilo* ("out of nothing"). I will hold to my argument above that the woman of Jesus's parable did represent *some* women in the society of his time, however few they may have been.

52

The Woman Who Anointed Jesus

EACH OF THE FOUR Gospels contains a story of a woman anointing Jesus with expensive ointment or perfume.[1] These stories have similarities in detail, but also numerous significant differences. For example, two have Jesus's head being anointed and two have his feet being anointed. Only in the Fourth Gospel is the woman named as Mary. And, despite the traditional association with Mary Magdalene, this is Mary of Bethany, sister of Martha and Lazarus. The "woman who was a sinner" (Luke 7:37) was somehow combined with the name Mary to yield Mary Magdalene.[2] Furthermore, this woman came to be identified with the woman taken in adultery as recorded in John 7:53—8:11.[3] This misidentification became entrenched in Christian tradition by a famous homily of Pope Gregory the Great (540-604 CE). "Pope Gregory positively identified the unnamed anointer and adulteress as Mary, and suggested that the ointment used on Jesus' feet was once used to scent Mary's body."[4]

We should note that nowhere in the text is Mary Magdalene referred to as a sinner, however, but as one from whom seven demons had gone

---

1. Matt 26:6-13, Mark 14:3-9, Luke 7:36-50.

2. For an excellent sketch showing how ancient is this misconception, see Knowles, *Let Her Be*, 159. For a more extended discussion, see Camery-Hoggatt, "Images of Mary Magdalene in Christian Tradition: A Case of Prostituted Identity," 19-23. Also, see above.

3. One of the most complicated textual problems of the entire New Testament concerns this passage. Some manuscripts of John omit it entirely; some omit, but leave space for it; some place it at the end of John: and a few place it in one of two locations in the Gospel of Luke. (For a concise discussion of this problem, see Kilgallen, *A Brief Commentary on the Gospel of John*, 95-97.) Depending on what translation one reads, this story may be bracketed, placed in a footnote, or relegated to the end of the Gospel of John, depending on the translators' conclusions regarding the textual problem.

4. Birger A. Pearson, "Did Jesus Marry?" 37.

out (Luke 8:2). Another false equation has been made—demon possession has been equated with sin, and sinner has been understood as prostitute.[5] "Sinner" and "prostitute" are not equivalent terms, by any standard of judgment.[6] Further, of the four accounts of the anointing, only Luke has any indication of the woman's character as a sinner.[7]

Obviously, to sort out the difficulties briefly set forth above is far beyond the scope of this study.[8] I will therefore limit my focus to what the woman does, and leave aside the issue of her identity or whether more than one woman may have anointed Jesus.

Just how much the anointing woman's actions deviated from what was considered proper in her society is captured well in the following passage from Swidler in his discussion of Luke's account of the anointing:

> First, in that culture one did not publicly speak to one's own wife, let alone to a strange woman, indeed a known "sinner," probably a prostitute! Jesus not only spoke with her but let her touch him and kiss him. Further, a woman was never to let her hair be uncovered, and to loose it in public was grounds for mandatory divorce; this woman uncovered her hair, loosed it, and wiped Jesus' feet with it, without thereby scandalizing Jesus—although Simon was clearly scandalized. Jesus rebuked the Pharisee and treated the woman not as a sexual creature but as a person; he spoke of her human and spiritual actions, her love, her unlove (her sins), her being forgiven, and her faith.[9]

More than one scholar has suggested that the story of Jesus's anointing was a prophetic action. This issue turns in part on whether Jesus's feet or head was anointed. Fiorenza argues that "it is much more likely that in the original story the woman anointed Jesus' head." She then goes

---

5. Cf. Swidler, *Biblical Affirmations of Woman*, 224, 275; Belleville, *Women Leaders and the Church*, 111: Bilezikian, *Beyond Sex Roles*, 90, 102; Parales, *Hidden Voices*, 33: F. Scott Spencer, *Dancing Girls*, 108. Contrast Getty-Sullivan, *Women in the New Testament*, 105.

6. For an idea of the breadth of meaning the word sinner could bear, see Fiorenza, *In Memory of Her*, 128. F. Scott Spencer notes that the first person labeled a sinner in Luke is Simon Peter, and that no one had ever accused him of being a gigolo or boy toy! (*Dancing Girls*, 108). Cf. also Getty-Sullivan, *Women in the New Testament*, 110–11.

7. Cf. Swidler, *Biblical Affirmations of Woman*, 207–8,

8. For a concise portrayal of the differences among the Gospel accounts, see the chart in Getty-Sullivan, *Women in the New Testament*, 107.

9. Swidler, *Biblical Affirmations of Woman*, 187.

The Woman Who Anointed Jesus

on to say, "Since the prophet in the Old Testament anointed the head of the Jewish king, the anointing of Jesus' head must have been understood immediately as the prophetic recognition of Jesus."[10] She also suggests that an anointing of Jesus's feet would have been so commonplace that it probably would not have been noticed.[11] In light of the above quote from Swidler, however, I would have to differ with Fiorenza. Anything that extraordinary would have been sufficient to catch the attention of everyone present. I am very sympathetic with Fiorenza's position on the whole, particularly in noting that the name of the "betrayer" of Jesus was retained, "but the name of the faithful disciple is forgotten because she was a woman."[12]

However one may read this story, a few things are rather clear. One is that a woman has defied the social roles that her society attempted to impose on her. Another is that she is not defined by a husband or any other male in her life. Further, she risked being branded as a prostitute because of her actions, whether or not she actually was. By being carefully contrasted with Simon the Pharisee she is an example of the "first becoming last and the last first." Jesus commended her actions as belonging to the Gospel wherever that Gospel should be preached. Of what male disciple could this be said—except for Judas Iscariot?!

---

10. Fiorenza, *In Memory of Her*, xiv. Cf. also Murphy, *The Word according to Eve*, 137. Some scholars have argued for two anointings, with two versions of each being recorded in the Gospels. Some further suggest that each had its own symbolism: the anointing on the head represented his being anointed as Messiah and King, and the anointing on the feet symbolizing his being anointed for his death and burial. See, for example, Albright and Freedman, gen eds., *The Gospel according to John I-XII*, 449–54; Parales, *Hidden Voices*, 38.

11. Fiorenza, *In Memory of Her*, xiv.

12. Ibid., xiii. For an excellent discussion of the anointing story as being one of boundaries between "insiders" and "outsiders," and Jesus's subversion of those boundaries, see Thurston, *Knowing Her Place*, 59–68.

53

The Elect Lady

THIS LADY IS MENTIONED only in the Christian Testament in the book we call Second John. The opening address reads, "The Elder to (an) Elect Lady (*eklektē kyria*)." Neither the author nor the addressee of this writing is further identified. Tradition has associated it with the apostle John, although the name is not found anywhere in 1–3 John. The "lady" has traditionally been assumed to be a metaphor for a church. Thomas E. Johnson represents this traditional view, saying, "The chosen lady and her children is the author's way of referring to a church and its members."[1]

On the other hand, going back as far as Clement of Alexandria (late second, early third centuries CE), the lady has been considered to be an actual historical individual. Clement further argued that she was a Babylonian woman whose name was Eclecta, rather than the latter being an adjective meaning "chosen" or "elect."[2] This argument is difficult to maintain, due to the final verse of 2 John in which an elect sister is mentioned. If "elect" is a proper name in verse 1, why not in verse 13? Then we would have two (undifferentiated) women by the same name in the same family.[3]

Whether or not we can know the woman's name or nationality, recent feminist scholars have increasingly argued for her identity as an

---

1. Gasque, New Testament ed., *1, 2, and 3 John*, 147. See also Grenz with Muirkjesbo, *Women in the Church*, 91; Hubbard and Barker, gen. eds., *1, 2, 3 John*, 316–19: Howard, *1, 2, & 3 John, Jude, Revelation*, 35; Raymond Brown, *The Gospel and Epistles of John*, 123: James Dunn, gen. ed., *The Theology of the Johannine Epistles*, 91–93; Tasker, gen. ed., *The Epistles of John*, 200–201: Bruce, *The Epistles of John*, 137; et al. For a more comprehensive discussion of the possibilities for interpreting the "elect lady," see Lindars, Edwards & Court, *The Johannine Literature*, 126–28.

2. Cf. Kraemer, *Her Share of the Blessings*, 176; 243 n. 19. Cf. also Parales, *Hidden Voices*, 71; Kraemer, *Her Share of the Blessing*, 177.

3. Cf. Morris, *The Lady Was a Bishop*, 1–2.

The Elect Lady

actual, historical person. Aida Besancon Spencer is representative of this viewpoint. In her argument for the woman as an individual, rather than a metaphor for a local church, she makes the following points:

1. *Kuria* ("lady") is the feminine of *kurios*, "lord" or "master"; hence she is in a position of authority.[4]
2. The author in 1 John addresses his recipients as "my little children," and so it is unlikely that he would refer to the same people as an elect lady.
3. The use of the plural "children" in verses 6–12 is best understood by seeing the woman as an individual and the "children" being adult members of her congregation.
4. *Kuria* has never been found as a metaphor for a congregation.

She then concludes by saying, "Readers today should not be at all surprised that 'the elect lady' was a woman overseeing a church in her house."[5] Morris makes the further claim that the "Elect Lady" was "an elected person ordained to a special service of the Christian community, that is, as overseer."[6] Grenz is more cautious, saying, "To date, the exegetical question has not been answered definitively. There are good reasons to see in this epistle support for the contention that the early congregations had women leaders. But the exegetical case is admittedly inconclusive."[7]

Perhaps it is worth noting here that even scholars as conservative as A. T. Robertson and Kenneth M. Wuest have affirmed that Second John is addressed to a distinguished woman. In Schmidt's words, "In all likelihood, the epistle was addressed to a female leader in the apostolic church, just as the opening verse of 3 John is addressed to a male leader."[8] Wuest further affirmed that her home was probably the meeting place of the local church.[9] Baptist Pastor Lamar Wadsworth gives this excellent summary of the "elect lady":

---

4. Cf. Knowles, *Let Her Be*, 165; Parales, *Hidden Voices*, 71: Stanton, *The Woman's Bible*, II:175; Grenz with Muirkjesbo, *Women in the Church*, 70–71.
5. Aida Besancon Spencer, *Beyond the Curse*, 109–12.
6. Morris, *The Lady Was a Bishop*, 2.
7. Grenz with Muirkjesbo, *Women in the Church*, 92.
8. Schmidt, *Veiled and Silenced*, 206.
9. Cited in Knowles, *Let Her Be*, 166.

Here in this little letter is all the Bible tells us about the chosen lady: John had the highest regard for her as a colleague in ministry. She was well-known among the churches to which 1 John was written. She was a gracious and loving person. She was so full of the Spirit of Christ that anyone who loved him would have to love her. She knew the difference between sound teaching and hogwash, and she was able to teach others the difference. Most people who were products of her ministry kept on walking in truth. That is all we know about her, but that is enough to uphold her as a worthy model for a church leader and as a biblical example of a Christian woman who engaged in public ministry that included teaching and preaching the word of God.[10]

---

10. Wadsworth, "Who Was the 'Chosen Lady' of 2 John?" 44. I will note in passing Wadsworth's assumption that the author's name was John, which is not supported by anything in the text, but only in later tradition.

54

Philip's Daughters

Even for women these daughters are perhaps the most underreported in the entire Bible. They get one offhand sentence in Acts 21:9: "Now to this man were four virgin daughters who prophesied (*prophēteuousai*)" [My translation]. Those familiar with the Greek language will note that *prophēteuousai* is a present participle, indicating ongoing, repeated, prophesying. And, for those who would make a distinction between preaching and prophesying, they are grasping at straws. Prophecy is not an English word at all, but a transliteration of the Greek word *prophasi*, which is the third person singular of a verb meaning "she/he speaks forth." It has nothing essentially to do with prediction of the future, although that may be involved. To prophesy is simply to speak forth the word of God, regardless of whether that word has to do with past, present, or future. (A good example of prophecy that speaks entirely of the past is Luke 2:67–74.) This point is made clear in S. F. Hunter's comment, "Luke records that Philip had 4 daughters who were preachers."[1] Wadsworth likewise uses the term preachers rather than prophets, saying, "Luke mentions them in Acts 21:4 [sic],[2] not because it was remarkable for a young single woman to be a preacher, but because it was remarkable for there to be four of them in one family."[3] In a similar vein Grady writes, "Philip's daughters were in essence women preachers who experienced a high level of respect for their spiritual insights and level of gifting."[4]

Some rather faint traces of the activities of these female prophets can be found in the writings of the Church Fathers. Eusebius, the first church

---

1. *The International Standard Bible Encyclopaedia*, s.v. "Philip, the Evangelist."
2. The correct verse is actually Acts 21:9.
3. Wadsworth, "Who Was the 'Chosen Lady' of 2 John?" 43.
4. Grady, *10 Lies the Church Tells Women*, 40.

historian, quotes Papias as saying that "he heard a wonderful tale from the daughters of Philip. For he relates that in his time one rose from the dead."[5] The same writer quotes one Proclus as saying, "Their tomb is there (Hierapolis) and the tomb of their father."[6] In another passage Eusebius says, "Among those (evangelists) that were celebrated at that time was Quadratus, who, report says, was renowned along with the daughters of Philip for his prophetical gifts."[7] Although the daughters are not specifically the source of this quotation, it is clear that the word "renowned" applied to both Quadratus (of whom little is known with any certainty) and the daughters of Philip. They were clearly renowned for their prophetic gifts.

Concerning these passages in Eusebius, Eisen writes,

> The history of reception allows us to conclude that in the early period these women were of great significance.... Especially significant in this report by Eusebius is that Philip's daughters appear as the authorities for a tradition; this shows that they were respected in early Christianity. The impression is augmented and strengthened by another reference in Eusebius's work. He quotes from a writing of Miltiades against the New Prophecy (Hist. eccl. 5.17.3–4) [sic]. Miltiades mentions the daughters of Philip as among the prophets of the New Covenant and emphasizes that the Montanist prophets are wrong to cite them as examples. This shows that the daughters of Philip were regarded, in the history of reception, as legitimate prophets of the New Covenant. Even Eusebius raises no objection to them.[8]

Fiorenza concludes from the same writings that the fame of Philip's daughters "was so great that the provinces of Asia derive their apostolic origin from them."[9] Parales sounds a similar note, saying, "According to Eusebius, a fourth-century bishop, these four daughters were responsible

---

5. *Church History*, iii.xxix.ix. It should be noted here that Eusebius was rather obviously confused concerning Philip, one of the original twelve apostles, and Philip the Evangelist as he is usually called. The latter was one of the seven chosen to minister to a group of widows who were being neglected (see Acts 7). See *The Nicene and Post-Nicene Fathers*, vol. 1, 162 n. 6, for an extended discussion of Eusebius's confusion of the two men.

6. Ibid., iii.xxxi.iv.

7. Ibid., iii.xxxvii.i.

8. Eisen, *Women Officeholders in Early Christianity*, 69.

9. Fiorenza, *In Memory of Her*, 299.

for much of the evangelization of Asia."[10] Reimer, more cautiously, states, "According to the passages just cited (Acts 6:5; 8:5, 26–40), these four prophets must belong to those who were driven out of Jerusalem. They have therefore taken part in the proclamation of the gospel.... It is possible that they were so well known that Luke could not avoid mentioning them."[11] Belleville suggests that the brevity of the mention of these prophets is due to the fact that female prophets were so well accepted in the early church as to make elaboration unnecessary.[12]

It did not take long for leaders of the church to begin trying to domesticate these daughters of Philip. "The women whom the mainstream Christian church of the first centuries C.E. still knew as prophets were domesticated in retrospect. This is what Hippolytus (late 2nd, early 3rd centuries C.E.) had to say about the evangelist Philip's four daughters who, according to Acts 21:8f. [sic], were prophets in Caesarea in the days of Paul: 'but they did not rise up against the men and stayed within the boundaries set for them.'"[13] Martin Luther perpetuated this position that, at best, can be labeled only as an argument from silence.[14] Knowles may be alluding to Hippolytus when he says that "some hierarchicalists have suggested that Philip's daughters prophesied in private but not in public." He then responds, "This is an absurd idea because the very nature of prophesying is communicating God's word to others."[15] Ruether presses the matter one step further and says, "The right to preach was given to women by the Holy Spirit at Pentecost, and women in the apostolic age, such as Anna and the daughters of Philip and Priscilla, taught in public. It is male tyranny against the explicit word of Scripture that has denied women the right to preach and has kept women from the education by which their superior gifts might be evident."[16]

---

10. Parales, *Hidden Voices*, 67. Parales may have claimed more here than the evidence will support. She references Fiorenza, *In Memory of Her*, 299, for this claim. Cf. Swidler, *Biblical Affirmations of Woman*, 302.

11. Reimer, *Women in the Acts of the Apostles*, 248.

12. Belleville, *Women Leaders and the Church*, 57. Cf. also Nunnally-Cox, *Foremothers*, 132.

13. Schottroff, *Lydia's Impatient Sisters*, 139.

14. Cf. Ruether, *Women and Redemption*, 121.

15. Knowles, *Let Her Be*, 158.

16. Ruether, *Women and Redemption*, 129.

Here we find four women who are defined solely by their role as prophets. Their father Philip is mentioned, to be sure, but there is not the slightest suggestion that he "covered" his daughters regarding their prophesying. The later traditions, few as they may be, further underscore this point. In Grenz's words, "In any case, for Luke, their involvement in prophesying clearly moved women such as Philip's daughters into the realm of authoritative utterance and beyond the traditional first-century roles of daughter, wife and mother."[17]

---

17. Grenz with Muirkjesbo, *Women in the Church*, 82.

Bibliography

Albright, William Foxwell, and David Noel Freedman, gen. eds. *Anchor Bible Commentary*. Vol. 29, *The Gospel according to John I-XII*, by Raymond Brown. Garden City: Doubleday, 1966.

Allen, Clifton J., gen. ed. *Genesis-Exodus*. Vol. 1 of *The Broadman Bible Commentary*, ed. Clifton J. Allen. Nashville: Broadman, 1969.

Anderson, Bernhard. *Understanding the Old Testament*, 4th ed. Englewood Cliffs: Prentice-Hall, 1986.

Armstrong, Karen. *In the Beginning: A New Reading of the Book of Genesis*. New York: Alfred A. Knopf, 1996.

Bach, Alice, ed. *The Pleasure of Her Text: Feminist Readings of Biblical and Historical Texts*. Philadelphia: Trinity, 1990.

Bal, Mieke. *Lethal Love: Feminist Literary Readings of Biblical Love Stories*. Bloomington: Indiana University, 1987.

———. *Murder and Difference: Gender, Genre, and Scholarship on Sisera's Death*. Translated by Matthew Gumpert. Bloomington: Indiana University, 1988.

Bar-Ilan, Meir. *Some Jewish Women in Antiquity*. Atlanta: Scholars, 1998.

Barclay, William. *The Gospel of Luke*. Philadelphia: Westminster, 1956.

———. *The Letter to the Romans*. Philadelphia: Westminster, 1957.

Barton, Ruth Haley. *The Truths that Free Us: A Woman's Calling to Spiritual Transformation*. Colorado Springs: WaterBrook, 2000.

Bauckham, Richard. *Gospel Women: Studies of the Named Women in the Gospels*. Grand Rapids: Eerdmans. 2002.

"Before Mary: The Ancestresses of Jesus." *Bible Review* XX, no. 6 (December, 2004): 13–23.

Belleville, Linda L. *Women Leaders and the Church: Three Crucial Questions*. Grand Rapids: Baker, 2000.

Bellis, Alice Ogden *Helpmates Harlots Heroes: Women's Stories in the Hebrew Bible*. Louisville: Westminster/John Knox, 1994.

Berquist, Jon L. *Reclaiming Her Story: The Witness of Women in the Old Testament*. St. Louis: Chalice, 1992.

Bilezikian, Gilbert. *Beyond Sex Roles*, 2d ed. Grand Rapids: Baker, 1985.

Blankenhorn, David, Don Browning, and Mary Stewart Van Leeuwen, eds. *Does Christianity Teach Male Headship?* Grand Rapids: Eerdmans, 2004.

Boldrey, Richard, and Joyce Boldrey. Foreword by David M. Scholer. *Chauvinist or Feminist: Paul's View of Women*. Grand Rapids: Baker, 1976.

Brenner, Athalya. *The Israelite Woman*. Sheffield: JSOT, 1994.

Brown, Cheryl Anne. *No Longer Be Silent: First Century Jewish Portraits of Biblical Women*. Louisville: Westminster/John Knox, 1992.

Bibliography

Brown, Raymond. *The Gospel and Epistles of John*. Collegeville: Liturgical, 1988.
Brown, Theron. *Nameless Women of the Bible*. New York: American Tract Society, 1904.
Bushnell, Katherine C. *God's Word to Women*, reprint ed. Oakland: Katherine C. Bushnell, 1930.
Byrne, Brendan. *Paul and the Christian Woman*. Collegeville: Liturgical, 1988.
Camery-Hoggatt, Jerry. "Images of Mary Magdalene in Christian History: A Case of Prostituted Identity." *Priscilla Papers* 18, no. 4 (Fall, 2004): 19–23
Carmody, Denise Lardner. *Biblical Woman: Contemporary Reflections on Scriptural Texts*. New York: Crossroad, 1992.
Carmody, John, Denise Lardner Carmody, and Robert L. Cohn. *Exploring the Hebrew Bible*. Englewood Cliffs: Prentice-Hall, 1988.
Caspi, Mishael Maswari, and Sascha Benjamin Cohen. *Still Waters Run Deep: Five Women of the Bible Speak*. New York: University Press of America, 1999.
Clark, Elizabeth A. *Women in the Early Church*. Collegeville: Liturgical, 1983.
Coffey, Kathy. *Hidden Women of the Gospels*. New York: Crossroad, 1996.
Cooey, Paula M. et al., eds. *Embodied Love: Sensuality and Relationship as Feminist Values*. San Francisco: Harper & Rowe, 1987.
Cross, Frank Moore. *From Epic to Canon: History and Literature in Ancient Israel*. Baltimore: Johns Hopkins, 1998.
Crossan, John Dominic, and Jonathan L. Reed. *In Search of Paul: How Jesus's Apostle Opposed Rome's Empire with God's Kingdom*. San Francisco: Harper San Francisco, 2004.
Croy, N. Clayton. "A Case Study in Translators' Bias." *Priscilla Papers* 115, no. 2 (Spring, 2001): 9.
Cunningham, Loren, and David J. Hamilton, with Janice Rogers. *Why Not Women?* Seattle: YWAM, 2000.
Day, Peggy L., ed. *Gender and Difference in Ancient Israel*. Minneapolis: Fortress, 1989.
de Boer, Esther. *Mary Magdalene: Beyond the Myth*. Harrisburg: Trinity Press International, 1997.
Deen, Edith. *All the Women of the Bible*. New York: Harper & Brothers, 1955.
del Mastro, M.L. *All the Women of the Bible*. Edison, NJ: Castle Books, 2004.
Diamant, Anita. *The Red Tent*. New York: Picador USA, 1997.
Dornisch, Loretta. *A Woman Reads the Gospel of Luke*. Collegeville: Liturgical, 1996.
Douglas, Jane Dempsey, and James F. Kay, eds. *Women, Gender and Christian Community*. Louisville: Westminster/John Knox, 1997.
Dunn, James D. G., ed. *New Testament Theology: The Theology of the Johannine Epistles*. Cambridge: Cambridge University, 1991.
Edersheim, Alfred. *The Life and Times of Jesus the Messiah*. Reprint ed. Peabody: Hendrickson, n.d.
Eisen, Ute E. *Women Officeholders in Early Christianity*. Collegeville: Liturgical, 2000.
Evans, Mary J. *Women in the Bible*. Downers Grove: Intervarsity, 1983.
Exum, J. Cheryl. *Fragmented Women*. Valley Forge: Trinity Press International, 1993.
Fiorenza, Elisabeth Schussler. *In Memory of Her: A Feminist Theological Reconstruction of Christian Origins*. New York: Crossroad, 1985.
———. *Sharing Her Word: Feminist Biblical Interpretation in Context*. Edinburgh: T & T Clark, 1998.
Franzmann, Martin H. *Romans*. St. Louis: Concordia, 1968.

Bibliography

Fuller, Reginald H. *The Formation of the Resurrection Narratives.* Philadelphia, Fortress, 1971.

Gaines, Janet Howe. "How Bad Was Jezebel?" *Bible Review* 16, no. 5 (October, 2000): 13-23.

Gasque, W. Ward. New Testament ed., *New International Bible Commentary.* Vol. 17, *1, 2, and 3 John,* by Thomas E. Johnson. Peabody: Hendrickson, 1993.

Getty-Sullivan, Mary Ann. *Women in the New Testament.* Collegeville: Liturgical, 2001.

Grady, J. Lee. *10 Lies the Church Tells Women.* Lake Mary, FL: Creation House, 2000.

———. *25 Tough Questions about Women and the Church.* Lake Mary, FL: Charisma House, 2003.

Grassi, Joseph A. *The Secret Identity of the Beloved Disciple.* New York: Paulist, 1992.

Grenz, Stanley J., with Denise Muirkjesbo. *Women in the Church: A Biblical Theology of Women in Ministry.* Downers Grove: Intervarsity, 1995.

Gritz, Sharon Hodgin. *Paul, Women Teachers, and the Mother Goddess at Ephesus.* New York: University Press of America, 1991.

Groothuis, Douglas. "What Jesus Thought about Women," *Priscilla Papers* 16, no.3 (Summer, 2002): 17-20.

Groothuis, Rebecca Merrill. *Good News for Women: A Biblical Picture of Gender Equality.* Grand Rapids: Baker, 1997.

Gundry, Patricia. *Woman Be Free.* Grand Rapids: Suitcase Books, 1977.

Hennecke, Edgar, Wilhelm Schneemelcher, and R. McL. Wilson, eds. *New Testament Apocrypha,* 2 vols. Translated by Walter Bauer et al. Eng. ed., Philadelphia: Westminster, 1963.

Howard, Fred D. *Layman's Bible Book Commentary.* Vol. 24, *1, 2, & 3 John, Jude, Revelation.* Nashville: Broadman, 1982.

Hubbard, David A., and Glenn W. Barker, eds. *Word Biblical Commentary.* Vol. 2, *Genesis 16-50.* Dallas: Word, 1994.

Hull, Gretchen Gaebelein. *Equal to Serve.* Old Tappan, NJ: Fleming H. Revell, 1987; Grand Rapids: Baker, 1998.

Jensen, Anne. *God's Self-Confident Daughters: Early Christianity and the Liberation of Women* (in German). Louisville: Westminster/John Knox, 1996.

Johnson, Alan F. "A Christian Understanding of Submission." *Priscilla Papers* 17, no. 4 (Fall, 2003): 11-20.

Keefe, Alice A. "Rapes of Women/Wars of Men." *Semeia* 61 (1993): 79-97.

Keener, Craig. *Paul, Women and Wives: Marriage and Women's Ministry in the Letters of Paul.* Peabody: Hendrickson, 1992.

Kenyon, Sir Frederic. *Our Bible and the Ancient Manuscripts.* New York: Harper & Row, 1958.

Knowles, Charles O. *Let Her Be: Right Relationships and the Southern Baptist Conundrum over Woman's Role.* Columbia: KnoWell, 2002.

Kraemer, Ross Shepard. *Her Share of the Blessings.* New York: Oxford University, 1992.

———, and Mary Rose D'Angelo, eds. *Women and Christian Origins.* New York: Oxford University, 1999.

Kroeger, Catherine Clark. "Does Belief in Women's Equality Lead to an Acceptance of Homosexual Practice?" *Priscilla Papers* 18, no. 2 (Spring, 2004): 3-10.

LaCocque, Andre. *The Feminine Unconventional: Four Subversive Figures in Israel's Tradition.* Minneapolis: Fortress, 1990.

Bibliography

Levine, Amy-Jill, ed. *"Women Like This": New Perspectives on Jewish Women in the Greco-Roman World*. Atlanta: Scholars, 1991.

Lightfoot, J. B. *Saint Paul's Epistles to the Colossians and to Philemon*. Reprint ed. Grand Rapids: Zondervan, 1959.

Lindars, Barnabas, Ruth B. Edwards, and John M. Court. *The Johannine Literature* Sheffield: Academic, 2000.

Lofts, Norah. *Women in the Old Testament: Twenty Psychological Portraits*. New York: Macmillan Company, 1949.

MacHaffie, Barbara J. *Her Story: Women in Christian Tradition*. Philadelphia: Fortress, 1986.

Marshall, I. Howard, W. Ward Gasque, and Donald A. Hagner, eds. *The New International Greek Commentary. The Epistles to the Colossians and to Philemon*. Grand Rapids: Eerdmans, 1996.

Martos, Joseph, and Pierre Hegy, eds. *Equal at the Creation: Sexism, Society, and Christian Thought*. Toronto: University of Toronto, 1998.

McKinlay, Judith E. *Gendering Wisdom the Host: Biblical Invitations to Eat and Drink*. Sheffield: Sheffield Academic, 1996.

Meyers, Carol. *Discovering Eve: Ancient Israelite Women in Context*. New York: Oxford University, 1988.

Moltmann-Wendel, Elisabeth. *The Women around Jesus*. Translated by John Bowden (in German). New York: Crossroad, 1982.

Morris, Joan. *The Lady Was a Bishop*. New York: Macmillan, 1973.

Murphy, Cullen. *The Word according to Eve: Women and the Bible in Ancient Times and Our Own*. New York: Houghton Mifflin, 1998.

Niditch, Susan. "Eroticism and Death in the Tale of Jael" in *Gender and Difference In Ancient Israel*. Edited by Peggy L. Day. Minneapolis: Fortress, 1989.

———. *Oral World and Written Word*. Louisville: Westminster/John Knox, 1996.

Nunally-Cox, Janice. *Foremothers: Women of the Bible*. New York: Seabury, 1981.

Nyland, Ann. "Papyri, Women, and Word Meaning in the New Testament." *Priscilla Papers* 17, no. 4 (Fall, 2003): 3–9.

Olson, Virgil. "A Tale of Two New Testament Couples." *Priscilla Papers* 15, no. 1 (Winter, 2001): 12–14.

Parales, Heidi Bright. *Hidden Voices: Biblical Women and Our Christian Heritage*. Macon: Smith and Helwys, 1998.

Para-Mallam, Funmi. "Recognition, Rewards, and Renewal in the Book of Ruth." *Priscilla Papers* 18, no. 1 (Winter, 2004): 13–19.

Pearson, Birger A. "Did Jesus Marry?" *Bible Review* XXI, no. 2 (Spring, 2005): 32–39, 47.

Pederson, Rena. *The Lost Apostle: Searching for the Truth about Junia*. San Francisco: Jossey-Bass, 2006.

Petersen, John. *Reading Women's Stories: Female Characters in the Hebrew Bible*. Minneapolis: Fortress, 2004.

Phelan, John E., Jr. "Women and the Aims of Jesus." *Priscilla Papers* 18, no. 1 (Winter, 2004): 7–11.

Preato, Dennis J. "A Female Apostle," *Priscilla Papers* 17, no. 2 (Spring, 2003): 23–25.

Ranft, Patricia. *Women and Spiritual Equality in Christian Tradition*. New York: St. Martin's, 1998.

Raschke, Carl A., and Susan Doughty Raschke. *The Engendering God: Male and Female Faces of God*. Louisville: Westminster/John Knox, 1995.

Bibliography

Reimer, Ivoni Richter. *Women in the Acts of the Apostles: A Feminist Liberation Perspective.* Translated by Linda M. Maloney (in German). Fortress: Minneapolis, 1995.

Reinhartz, Adela. "Women in the Johannine Community." Pages 14–33 in *A Feminist Companion to John*, vol. 2. Edited by Amy-Jill Levine. Cleveland: Pilgrim, 2003.

Rendsberg, Gary A. "Unlikely Heroes: Women as Israel." *Bible Review* 19, no. 1 (February, 2003): 16–23, 52.

Richards, Sue, and Larry Richards. *Every Woman in the Bible.* Nashville: Thomas Nelson, 1999.

Roberts, Benjamin Titus. *Ordaining Women—Biblical and Historical Insights.* Reprint edition. Indianapolis: Light and Life Publications, 1992 and 1997.

Ruether, Rosemary Radford. *Women and Redemption.* Minneapolis: Fortress, 1998.

Sakenfeld, Katharine Doob. *Deborah, Jael and Sisera's Mother: Reading the Scriptures in a Cross-Cultural Context."* Pages 12–22 in *Women, Gender & Christian Community.* Edited by James Dempsey Douglass and James F. Kay. Louisville: Westminster/John Knox, 1997.

Sayers, Dorothy L. *Are Women Human?* Grand Rapids: Eerdmans, 1971.

Scanzoni, Letha Dawson, and Nancy A Hardesty. *All We're Meant to Be*, 3rd ed. Grand Rapids: Eerdmans, 1992.

Schaberg, Jane. "Before Mary: The Ancestresses of Jesus." *Bible Review* XX, no. 6 (December, 2004), 13–23.

Schaff, Philip, and Henry Wace, eds. *A Select Library of Nicene and Post-Nicene Fathers of the Christian Church.* Translated by Arthur Cushman McGiffert. Vol.1, *The Church History of Eusebius.* Reprint edition. Grand Rapids: Eerdmans, 1976.

Schmidt, Alvin John. *Veiled and Silenced: How Culture Shaped Sexist Theology.* Macon: Mercer University, 1989.

Schottroff, Luise. *Lydia's Impatient Sisters: A Feminist Social History of Early Christianity.* Louisville: Westminster/John Knox, 1995.

———. "Important Aspects of the Gospel for the Future." Pages 205–10 in *What Is John: Readers and Readings in the Fourth Gospel*, no. 3. Edited by Fernando F. Segovia. Atlanta: Scholars Press, 1996.

Spencer, Aida Besancon. *Beyond the Curse: Women Called to Ministry.* Nashville: Thomas Nelson, 1985.

Spencer, F. Scott. *Dancing Girls, Loose Ladies, and Women of the Cloth: The Women in Jesus' Life.* New York: Continuum, 2004.

Stanton, Elizabeth Cady. *The Woman's Bible.* Reprint edition. Boston: Northeastern University, 1993.

Summers, Ray. *Commentary on Luke.* Waco: Word, 1973.

Swidler, Leonard. *Biblical Affirmations of Woman.* Philadelphia: Westminster, 1979.

Thurston, Anne. *Knowing Her Place: Gender and the Gospels.* New York: Paulist, 1998.

Tillman, William M., Jr. "Southern Baptists and Women in Ministry." *Priscilla Papers* 14, no. 3 (Summer, 2000): 13–16.

Trible, Phyllis. *God and the Rhetoric of Sexuality.* Philadelphia: Fortress, 1978.

———. *Texts of Terror: Literary-Feminist Readings of Biblical Narratives.* Philadelphia: Fortress, 1964.

———. et al. *Feminist Approaches to the Bible.* Washington: Biblical Archaeology Society, 1995.

Wadsworth, Lamar. "Who was the 'Chosen Lady' of 2 John?" *Priscilla Papers* 12, no. 1 (Winter, 1998): 40–44.

Bibliography

Walker, Williston. *A History of the Christian Church*. Revised by Cyril C. Richardson, Wilhelm Pauck, and Robert T. Handy. New York: Charles Scribner's Sons, 1959.

Warren, Brenda Griffin. "A Woman's Work." *Priscilla Papers* 17, no. 2 (Spring, 2003): 7–12.

Wedderburn, A. J. M. *Beyond Resurrection*. Peabody: Hendrickson, 1999.

Weems, Renita J. *Just a Sister Away: A Womanist Vision of Women's Relationships in the Bible*. San Diego: LuraMedia, 1988.

Wiley, Tatha. *Paul and the Gentile Women: Reframing Galatians*. New York: Continuum, 2005.

Winter, Miriam Therese. *Women of the Old Testament Knowledge Cards*. Rohnert Park, CA: Pomegranate Communications, n.d.

Witherington, Ben III. "Joanna: Apostle of the Lord—or Jailbait?" *Bible Review* XXI, no. 2 (Spring, 2005): 12–14, 46.

Yee, Gale A. "By the Hand of a Woman: The Metaphor of the Woman Warrior in Judges 4." *Semeia* 61 (1993): 99–132.

———. *Poor Banished Children of Eve: Woman as Evil in the Hebrew Bible*. Minneapolis: Fortress, 2003.

www.ingramcontent.com/pod-product-compliance
Lightning Source LLC
Chambersburg PA
CBHW062037220426

43662CB00010B/1535